Paul Keddy

If I Should Die Before You Wake

Instructions on the Art of Life

Published by
Creative Bound Inc.
P.O. Box 424, Carp, Ontario
Canada K0A 1L0
(613) 831-3641

ISBN 0-921165-48-X
Printed and bound in Canada
© 1997 Paul A. Keddy

Book design by Wendelina O'Keefe

Canadian Cataloguing in Publication Data

Keddy, Paul A., 1953-
    If I should die before you wake : instructions on the
art of life

ISBN 0-921165-48-X

    1. Self-actualization. 2. Spirituality. I. Title.

BJ1581.2.K42 1997   158.1   C97-900632-5

Contents

Preface

We all want to be happy, but it sometimes seems that the more we struggle to achieve happiness, the more we encounter pain. How, then, can we live a meaningful life and die without regret?

We may believe that the only way to experience such a thing is to escape our ordinary life and flee to an exotic tropical country where they speak a foreign language and eat strange foods. Perhaps we will decide instead to accept a miserable life and blame our family or our society for making it so. Or we may turn to a tradition that requires obedience to a particular authority figure or book. Alternatively, we may decide to indulge ourselves and try to stop thinking about our life at all. All of these could be seen as natural expressions of our desire to be happy. But they could also be ways to avoid the actual experience of our own lives.

There is another way. It is possible to live in a manner that is simple, full, rich, genuine and awake. It is possible to live a life in which we express all that is best about being human. It is possible to live in a way that leaves the world better for our having been here. And best of all, it is possible to start here, now, where we are. We do not need to reject the ordinary, mundane details of everyday life in order to encounter enlightenment. The busy day-to-day life of a western householder can be transformed into a spiritual path, not by hoping for a holiday, not by praying for a miracle, not by planning for early retirement, but by *waking up* to appreciate who we are. Here. Now.

It may seem remarkable that such a thing could be so. Perhaps we are sceptical, and decide to wait a little longer to check it out. Maybe next week, maybe next year, maybe after we graduate or get a job or retire. But as time passes we may find that the habits that caused our initial dissatisfaction with life only intensify. And at the end of it all lies death. Impending death may only heighten the all-pervading sense of frustration and suffering that daily erodes our confidence.

This book arose when my own death was approaching. I was determined to record for my two young sons some basic teachings on life, some few instructions that I wanted them to have when they entered adulthood. What, I wondered, were the few most basic principles of living that could be left for them? Gail Baird at Creative Bound encouraged me to express these in a way that would be accessible for everyone, son or daughter, child or adult. After all, each of us faces the same daily task of growing up in difficult times. And so the book for my sons grew into this version.

In their original form, many of these teachings were a precious gift from the Buddhist meditation master, poet and scholar, Chogyam Trungpa Rinpoche. But he was born in Tibet, trained as a great reincarnated teacher, and driven by a Communist invasion to become a penniless refugee in North America. I, in contrast, was born in North America, raised in a Christian society, and trained as a sceptical scholar.

If there was one thing that Chogyam Trungpa Rinpoche never tired of repeating, it was that the desire to escape to somewhere exotic is just another way of avoiding life. The body of teachings that he treated as his most precious legacy was the means by which we could transform ordinary western life into a journey of enlightenment. When he presented these teachings, he gave up his Buddhist robes, donned a western business suit, and even took a new name. It appeared that he was determined to express in every way possible that spirituality does not reside in any particular single tradition or any single culture.

Of course, if it were all that easy to transform our hectic daily life into a spiritual path, we would all be enlightened by now. But the art of living, like the art of war, is passed on from one human being to another. Who taught us how to sew? How to repair an engine? How to read? How to bake a cake? It was another human being. In the same way, we need someone to introduce us to the inner world of thoughts, feelings and emotions. We have a terrible shortage of such teachers in the West. Just as a house is built of bricks, boards, drywall, windows and nails, life is put together from elements such as hope, fear, happiness, despair, anger, frustration, duty and joy. If we lack a blueprint, if we have no contractor, if we have never met an architect, then we may never know what it is like to live in a real house. We may find ourselves huddled in a cave or a mud hut, all the while surrounded by beautiful building materials.

In this short book we are introduced to some basic elements of human experience. Each of these elements can be a vehicle that helps us wake up to a genuine human existence, or a millstone that weighs us down into further delusion. A skilled teacher can help us work with our actual day-to-day human experiences of fear, anger and joy, just as a contractor can help us build a solid foundation, frame a house, or repair a leaky roof. Each essay here is grounded in the instructions I received from Trungpa Rinpoche and from his son, Sakyong Mipham Rinpoche. But instructions are of little use if they cannot be applied to our own lives. And so, switching from building to baking, each essay can also be thought of as a cake. It may have been mixed with their recipe, but it was baked in a North American oven under my supervision. I have tried to share the recipe with you and comment on how to use it in our own culture, our own times and our own homes. In this regard I must also thank other senior cooks for their advice: Mr. Henry Chapin, Mr. Palden MacLennan, Khenpo Sonam Rinpoche and Professor John Dourly. If the cake is occasionally burned, however, that is my fault, not the fault of the recipe, my instructors or my advisors.

Life is workable. As human beings we all have a basic decency. If we take the time to experience our hopes and fears, we can wake up from frustration into enlightenment. Trungpa Rinpoche devoted his life to showing us it was so, to planting such ideas and the path to accomplish them here in the West. But as he once said, it is one thing to read the recipe, and quite another to get into the kitchen and bake the bread.

Throughout this book, reference is made to developing a sense of mindfulness, awareness and appreciation. This is grounded in the practice of sitting meditation, such as we may have seen in photographs of a Zen monastery. It would not be appropriate to give formal meditation instructions here. First, they are not easy to put into words. Second, meditation instructions are traditionally passed directly from one person to another. Finally, a book is like a tour guide to another country; it cannot substitute for the actual experience of being there. Indeed, the very word meditation is explosive. People have so many pre-conceived notions of what it might be. And so many possible forms of it are available, frequently from teachers with doubtful training. Often we may be attracted to the most exotic, when in fact what we need is the most basic. If you wish to expand these readings with the actual practice of mediation, may I suggest that you keep it simple. The most basic form of meditation is mindfulness-awareness meditation (or shamatha-vipashnya). This practice does not require focusing our attention on a single object like a candle. It does not allow us to experience union with some higher deity. It will not help us fly. It is not a form of worship. It does not involve closing the eyes and listening to nice music to create a peaceful realm. Rather, we take our posture in a relaxed, but formal way, and we even keep our eyes open. We then apply a simple means of relating with the breath that helps us avoid getting caught up in habitual patterns of thought. We find that we can remain still and somewhat detached from the habitual stories we tell ourselves about our life. We discover, perhaps to our surprise, that much of the time we are not experiencing the world at all. Instead of experiencing the world, we are often just talking to ourselves, or else replaying our favourite mental video tapes. Meditation, then, does not involve trying to hide from the world, nor does it manipulate reality. Rather, we are training our mind to experience the world simply for what it is. We are learning to discriminate between our beliefs about the world, and the direct experience of the world. In the appendix of this book there are instructions if you should wish to go further with the practice of meditation.

Starting Out

Peace
Spirituality
Confidence
Fear

...

Peace

*P*lease stop the rat race. Please get everyone off my back. Please let me feel good about myself. Please stop the wars. Please stop the mail, the phone, the fax, and the net. Please stop the brutality. Please clean up my bathroom. Please stop the constant irritation. Please make me well. Please love me for who I am. Please just leave me alone. Please just let me have some peace.

If only we *could* be at peace!

If only we had money without having to work. If only we could live in a cozy little cottage with a pleasant garden, neatly mowed lawn and white picket fence. This is what my mother wanted, to judge from a cushion she embroidered in her childhood; what *she* got was the Second World War. We could update her embroidery by adding the essential elements of a modern suburb: a neatly herbicided lawn, dwarf junipers, a riding lawn mower and two cars in the driveway. If only we could have these things, we know in our hearts that we would be at peace.

There seems to be this natural human tendency to want a cozy little nest or a dank little cave to hang out in. Perhaps this very tendency misleads us. Perhaps peace is not found by hiding out in a dream home in a cozy reclining chair. Perhaps it is not found in a log cabin weaving macramé hangers for spider plants while drinking herbal tea. Although we may try to create such worlds, these styles of peace, and the struggles to protect them, often turn out to be prisons. At best we have created an illusory world that puts us to sleep and lulls us into lethargy. At worst, the very struggle to get rid of the messy, dirty, unwanted parts of life becomes part of our problem. This desire to make a cozy nest seems to have its dark side: it is actually a private little war in which we try to shut out the world and seal ourselves off from the larger view of human circumstances.

Part of the problem may be that we blame ourselves for our misery. We may think the lack of peace is our own fault. Yet, when we look around us, surely we are wrong. Everybody else is actually in the same turmoil. Dissatisfaction with life, continual struggle to make it to the next day, these are not personal problems, these are a common human experience. Whatever is happening to us is happening to everyone else as well. The person who hurts us, the co-worker who spreads harmful gossip, the driver on the bus who is rude, the boss who insults us, the neighbor who steals from us, all of these people are in pain too. Perhaps their behavior is their own deluded attempt to make a peaceful nest for themselves.

If dissatisfaction and struggle are something that we share with everyone else, then we can let go of the hope that something simple and easy will magically give us peace. If we could buy that nice cottage, we might lie awake and worry about the leaky roof. If we could get that better job, our new boss might be a jerk. If we go back to school, we might find we have no time to spend with our family. There may be no strategy to escape. So what are we to do?

Well, even the realization that it is not just us may in itself be delightful, even liberating. Whatever is going on is not our fault; it is a human condition.

Do we really want to try to make a peaceful nest, if it will cause us further dissatisfaction, worry and struggle? If not, do we just give up and resign ourselves to a life of irritation and misery? Neither of these seems to be a very satisfactory solution. What are we to do?

One of the oldest books of western civilization, *The Odyssey*, addresses this very dilemma. *The Odyssey* begins at the end of the Trojan war. Odysseus is living with the sea nymph Calypso who has promised him immortality if he stays with her in her cave. Immortality with a sea nymph in a cave seems to be quite a cozy situation. But instead, Odysseus, a hero from the Trojan War, decides to sail home and reclaim his kingdom and his queen. He gathers his crew and sets sail. He soon encounters the lotos-eaters. The lotos-eaters have no memories and no aspirations, and when one of his crew eats lotos, the sailor forgets his home, his family and his country; he longs only for the endless empty dreams of nothingness. The ancient poets clearly believed that peace was not to be found in such lethargy or in a cozy cocoon, yet here we are millennia later still seeking peace in the cave of the sea nymph and the land of the lotos. Perhaps it is time, like Odysseus, to sail bravely forth, risking our lives if necessary, to rediscover our homeland and reclaim our wealth. Anything less is pissing away the gift of human existence.

Let us therefore redefine peace: peace is to be found in the skillful and determined application of our talents to waking up to our lives, and to the service of humankind.

How is it that an enlightened human search for better conditions somehow becomes degraded into a mere struggle for coziness and fear of relating to the world as it is? It appears that this search for peace is not quite as straightforward as we first hoped. Perhaps we have to go back to the beginning. What is it that we really want when we seek peace?

Confusion arises partly because the word peace has many meanings. It is not just the absence of war. Nor is it just a roof over our head and three square meals a day without a debt collector at the door. Most North Americans now have all of these, but dissatisfaction and even misery still hang like a cloud over our cities. Having the necessities and toys of the external world even approximately in order does not seem to be enough; otherwise, the suburbs would be heaven.

The peace we want so badly seems to be inner peace. Inner peace: these are easy words to write. But determining what they really mean is far more difficult. Our English language has so few words to describe the world of inner experience. It may be we are using the word peace in such a careless way that it only confuses us. Our culture is built around modification and control of the external world; we live in an industrial and technological society. Our vocabulary reflects this. If we had been raised Tibetan, we might not be able to operate a microwave or a computer, but we would have a rich vocabulary to describe our inner experiences. Perhaps we would be less unhappy if we even had the correct words to describe our misery and our hope.

Still, we torture ourselves into believing that inner peace is possible. If only we could keep the kitchen clean, get along with our spouse, win the lottery, write a best-selling book, find a job, floss three times a day, kick the habit, buy a house, pay off the mortgage…we know we would then be at peace. And we would be wrong. The First Noble Truth of Buddhism is that desire, dissatisfaction, and feelings of failure are a universal human experience. It is not that there is something wrong with you, or with me. It is not our fault (well, not quite) that everything is out of synchronization. All of us feel this way. This is the shared misery of being human.

The Buddha's fundamental insight into this was to see that the belief in something called peace, the craving for it, the assumption that someone exists to feel it, and the constant frenetic effort to produce it, are all tied up into a terrible cycle of suffering called *samsara*. The more we struggle for peace, the more elusive it becomes. The more we struggle, the stronger the cravings become. The more we struggle, the more we begin to believe that there is a self who can attain something. From one point of view, then, the very process of trying to find peace stirs up the water and raises clouds of mental confusion. And yet, at the same time, it is this urge that drives us forward towards greater possibilities.

We all want peace. But we have been sidetracked onto roads that are dead ends. The more we thrash about lost in the bushes, the more we exhaust and frustrate ourselves. We have been conditioned to believe that we can find peace if we just work harder. We have been deluded into thinking we can find peace if we just pray harder. We have been confused into thinking we can find peace if we do the same as the other people on our street. We have been discouraged into feeling that we lack the necessary wisdom and courage when in fact it is our human birthright. There is a path, a network of paths, an open highway, a multi-lane expressway to find personal peace and to cultivate enlightened beings in an enlightened society. To start, we have to explore the nature of our own minds and our own hearts. It is that easy, and it is that hard.

Spirituality

s human beings we all aspire to live lives that are full, rewarding and happy. And yet we continually seem to struggle with feelings of emptiness, frustration and misery. There appears to be an ongoing conflict between our aspiration for a meaningful life and our experience of daily struggle.

Frequently we try to resolve this conflict and ease our confusion by involving ourselves in all manner of philosophical speculations, by searching for an exotic escape from reality, by blaming society or our family, or by giving complete obedience to various authority figures and texts. There is an option that is much more practical: we simply start where we are and examine our own lives. Where else, after all, *could* we start? This life is all we have.

If we start here, with our own lives, what we do know is that we are alive, that people around us are alive, and that both pleasant and painful experiences arise in our lives. None of these are theories—they are just simple facts that we can see for ourselves. Our path, our spiritual path if you prefer, starts simply with the inquisitiveness and courage to experience these for just what they are. We may then extend the task to easing the suffering and confusion of others. This path is hardly a new idea. But it is an eminently practical one.

Sometimes we try to avoid these issues entirely. We try to hide from our conflict and frustration. We may try not to think about such matters at all, and instead concentrate upon the details of our life. We may hope that if we keep our mind full and busy, the conflict and dissatisfaction will go away. Perhaps we really believe that if we ignore our lives, somehow we will attain freedom at fifty-five on a sand beach somewhere. But if we attempt this strategy, we find that in spite of our best efforts, however much we concentrate, confusion and pain still find a way to get through our defenses. Perhaps we hit middle age, or become ill, or lose our job, or simply get old, and then all the issues we tried to hide from surge forward demanding our attention. Maybe we actually do retire at fifty-five and find that sitting on a sand beach overlooking the ocean only allows all our questions to rise like sea monsters. The very energy we put into hiding from our thoughts and feelings can rebound upon us like a boomerang.

What we need, then, is a guide to help us work directly and skillfully with our difficult lives. We need advice from other people who have done so. It is not quite like hiring a mechanic, a plumber, or electrician; at least we can look them up in the telephone directory. We want personal advice from people who can help us wake up, who can befriend us as we begin to reconnect with the phenomenal world. We could call such people "warriors."

The tradition of warriorship can be found in Japanese samurai traditions, in the North American Indian culture, in European medieval chivalry or in the legendary Shambhala kingdom of

Tibet. This kind of warriorship is not one of aggression, conflict, destruction, or imposition of one's views on others. A warrior, rather, is someone who faces death daily in an uncertain world, and yet has the courage to be a simple decent human being. This courage allows us to relax just a little and experience our life for what it really is. It may be as simple as the courage to experience raising a child in a slum, struggling daily for basic food. It may be the courage to stand up to tyranny when a dreadful death will result. It may be the courage to exercise self-restraint when others are indulging in their passions. It may be the courage to express passion in a world that preaches self-restraint. It may be the courage to found a new political party. Or it may be the courage to fight for humane policy changes in an established party. It is the courage to wake up to the actual experience of being a father, mother, poet, fire-fighter, pilot, scholar, engineer, soldier or monk.

If we decide to approach our life in this manner, we are following an ancient tradition that has served human beings well. On one hand, then, it is a well-worn path. Other people have woken up before us. We can draw upon their advice to guide us. On the other hand, the path is a lonely one. Each of us has to step onto it our own way, and each person's story is a unique one. While there may therefore be a sense of belonging to a spiritual tradition, there is no strict sense of regimentation, no insistence that one has to experience the world a certain way. There are most certainly disciplines required, but there is no single predetermined way to wake up or to express warriorship.

An essential element of warriorship is making friends with ourselves. As that is accomplished, our relationship with the world becomes relaxed, natural, and less fearful. It is difficult to make our way in the world if we are at war with ourselves. But making friends with ourselves is a spiritual challenge. We may find that some parts of our life just seem too painful to face; why bother to get to know ourselves at all? Further, most of us have been raised in traditions, religious or scientific, where we regard ourselves as fundamentally flawed and sinful. At this point, however, we are going to ease up on judging ourselves so harshly. We could begin to gently but courageously experience everything in our life, good and bad, happy and sad, painful and joyful. But we could accept these experiences without giving them the heavy labels of good and bad, without judging, without giving in to self-loathing, without trying to attack ourselves. We could begin this path by treating our self as a guest in our own home; we could try to get to know the guest before we launch on our great plan to reform them. Maybe we would find that our very desire to reform this guest is a big source of conflict. Perhaps we are not so bad as we really think. If there is a proclamation for the path of warriorship, it is exactly this. Human beings have a remarkable natural resourcefulness and a basic intention to lead decent and meaningful lives. We already have the seeds of enlightenment within us. The qualities of warriorship, of enlightenment, will naturally sprout and grow if we just give them the opportunity.

Much of the conflict of the world seems to be caused by self-hatred. Many of us may be expressing our lack of trust in our enlightened nature by trying to destroy parts of ourselves that we don't like, but all too often we end up doing so in a deluded way by harming other beings. The television evangelist who preaches the destruction of evil is perhaps afraid of his own darkness. The industrialist who destroys nature may not appreciate the value of his own wildness.

What would happen if we took the time to appreciate ourselves as we are? What resources might we naturally possess that we have never taken the time to find? In the Buddhist tradition we are told that the jewel of enlightenment is buried right in the midst of our own juicy manure. The regular practice of sitting meditation can provide an unbiased opportunity to discover ourselves. If we are not doing a formal meditation practice, we can pay attention to our own thoughts and feelings as they arise, without holding onto them too tightly. We can watch our experiences rise and fall away. It is not easy at first, but then neither was it easy to ride a bicycle the first time we tried. We can just start over and over again. We begin to develop a certain sense of balance. We begin to see what a rich heritage human beings possess. We also encounter a lot of manure. But as every gardener knows, manure is needed to grow a vigorous and productive garden.

A big potential obstacle to any spiritual path is arrogance. If we are certain that we are right, if we want to convert others, if we are unduly proud of our spiritual accomplishments, if we find ourselves following someone who tells us we are part of a select few, we should be aware that these are all signs of danger. We may have strayed off the path and into the ditch! Climb out again. Remember the Buddhist saying, 'If you meet the Buddha on the road, kill him.' This (outrageous) statement warns us that if our spirituality is becoming solid, if it is becoming an ego trip, then it is time to let go of it. If we believe that we have met the Buddha on the road, then we are missing the point of being Buddhist. If we feel it is necessary to prove to everyone that we are an impeccable warrior, then we may not yet be one.

If we are intrigued by this prospect of applying the principles of warriorship to our life, we need further instructions. The following essays introduce aspects of warriorship and spirituality that arise naturally in our day-to-day lives. All of these essays are intended as utterly practical instructions. Such instructions exist to help us appreciate life; none of them is intended to be yet another stick with which to beat ourselves. We could also avoid too much idle speculation. This is a practical, personal path. It is a raw, experiential path. There are no easy answers. Indeed, at times, the advice we receive may seem self-contradictory. If it seems this way, we may wish to recall the Zen master who was asked by his students why his advice seemed contradictory. "Sometimes you tell us one thing, sometimes it seems you say the exact opposite." "Well," he replied, "walking a spiritual path is like walking along a road on a foggy night. It is easy to fall into the ditch. Of course, if you do fall into the ditch, there is no choice but to climb back out and start over. The role of a teacher is simple. We have walked the road already, and can somewhat see through the fog. So sometimes you veer left, and I yell "Go right, go right"; sometimes you veer right and I must yell "Go left, go left."

May you be inspired to step onto the path of warriorship. May you have the courage to climb back out of the ditch. May you find a master warrior to shout directions in the fog.

Confidence

In my career as a professor, those students who were most difficult to work with were those who lacked confidence. Often they appeared to have a fortunate existence—good home, money, basic intelligence, friends, health. But they could not do anything with their situation because they lacked confidence. They were spinning their wheels, confused by what was happening around them, unable to act on their own behalf or anyone else's.

When we see that some people appear to have a lot of confidence, and others seem to lack it, it is easy for us to believe that confidence is something we gradually acquire, that it is a trick we learn, or that it is something we possess in proportion to the amount of money we inherit. No doubt it helps to have money, education, fine clothes, and trustworthy friends. But many of these may be a consequence rather than a cause of confidence.

When we talk about confidence, by the way, we are not talking about pumping ourselves up with adrenaline. We are not talking about chanting loudly and hurling insults, like at a sports event.

This kind of confidence is based upon fear. We are not talking about trying to pull some sort of con job on ourselves, to try to convince ourselves of something we don't really believe. Trying to pump up this kind of so-called confidence would only increase the confusion. Real confidence, the kind that we are talking about, is already present; it is part of our human inheritance. This kind of confidence is gentle, restrained, even sad. We could be confident building a house, even as we know that it will one day be a ruin. We could be confident in our caring for a child, even as we know that one day each child too will die.

It could be argued that bringing up the topic of confidence so early is quite dangerous. Perhaps someone will read this and confuse their confidence with their aggression. Perhaps they will assume that they can struggle forward in life by pushing others out of the way. Raising the topic of confidence has this risk, but then many of us are already using this deluded strategy. We are like the knight who assumes that with a bigger sword and sharper spurs, the battle will be won.

Perhaps others will hear about this unconditional confidence and be intimidated. We may believe that confidence is something that we will never possess. We may be unwilling to admit that like everyone else we have inherited a horse and saddle and sword. We may be irritated by the very suggestion that we have primordial confidence because of the implication that we are then expected to do something with it. It may be that we find it easier to believe that we are just a victim of circumstances beyond our control.

This is not to leave the impression that confidence requires combat. A mounted warrior does not need to constantly attack. We are talking about something quite different. The real warrior is the one who achieves victory without conflict. The real warrior has studied the balance of power, and aligns his forces with the landscape. Perhaps the mere display of gentleness and courage are often sufficient to be victorious.

Instead of trying to find the origin of confidence, instead of speculating further about it, we could just make a simple observation: the knight with rusty armor, dull sword, bedraggled horse and dirty face is defeated before the battle starts. Our attitude towards our life can influence our experiences. This is the reason why we encourage children to put on clean clothes, eat breakfast and wash their faces before going to school. We can rouse our confidence by wearing good clothes, eating good food, and sharing companionship. In the same way, the space around us can be treated as sacred. A knight does not pee in the castle corridors and spit on the king's carpets. An office or home can reflect this principle. The art we display, the chair we sit on, and the carpets we choose, all can reflect the radiance of a king's court.

Confidence is attracted to the knight who is prepared to accept it. But beware of mere ostentation. The knight who is too dependent upon gold cups, consorts, wine and tents is also on the road to defeat. Roman soldiers called their baggage 'impedimenta' for good reason.

Ultimately, let me assure you that the experience of confidence comes from nowhere in particular. It is simply part of our inheritance as a human being. We are all born with Buddha nature, with unconditioned confidence. The reason we are not all Buddhas is that desires, conflicting emotions, and fears arise like thick clouds and obscure the sun of our primordial confidence. Whatever situations arise, whatever our circumstances, remember that we cannot lose our confidence. Whether we are a modern day king (we call them Chief Executive Officers now), an imprisoned poet, a single parent, or a nameless bureaucrat, confidence can be found. It may *feel* lost, we may have lost sight of it, but it will always be there for us. If it feels lost, meditation cushions are there to help us rediscover it.

Fear

Everyone feels fear. So, when we find ourselves feeling fear, we do not need to worry that there is something wrong. A coward is someone who is afraid to admit fear, to himself or to others. To be brave, we have to recognize our constant fear. As long as we can feel our fear on a moment-to-moment basis, we know that we are alive.

My own two boys were fearless. This brought out everyone else's fears. At picnics they were always the ones off in the woods climbing trees, down at the lake throwing in stones, or trying to stoke the fire to make it burn higher and brighter. Other parents would light and stoke their own children's fears. "Don't climb that tree, dear. You might fall. Don't go near the water, darling. You might get wet. Don't put sticks in the fire, son. You might get burned. Stay near mummy and daddy." It is apparent that if children do not have enough of their own fears and insecurities, parents will be only too glad to provide them. There were many disapproving looks from other parents who felt I was being irresponsible to not inspire more fear in my sons. How much of the fear that we feel is just somebody else's fear that we were once force-fed?

Some parents seem to like fear in their children because it makes them easier to control. Fearless children seem to rouse their parents' hidden fears. But fear can prevent us from living. We may be afraid to go to school, afraid to leave the ghetto, afraid to challenge our parents, afraid to be who we are. If we allow fear to rule our lives, we might as well be in prison.

There is a large pond outside our house. It has brought so much pleasure into our lives. Migrating waterfowl. Great blue herons stalking fish. Choruses of frogs in the spring and summer. Reflection of autumn colours. Glimpses of basking turtles. Skating in the winter. Coyote tracks across the ice. Yet more than one visitor said that they would not be able to live with the fear of having a pond like that near their house. What if a child were to drown in it? If they could not tolerate the fear of a beaver pond in their lives, how desperately poor they must have been. Think how many other experiences and challenges were utterly beyond their reach.

Not everyone is afraid of beaver ponds, thankfully. But a great and nearly universal source of fear in our lives is fear of other people. We can fear loss of other people's attention. The class goofball who always has some way of drawing attention to himself is acting out of this fear. Or, we can fear being noticed at all. People around you who shy away from presenting their views may be afraid of your attention. The desire for approval is a powerful source of fear. The good little boys who always behave and always get good grades may be doing so not out of vision or joy, but out of fear of losing the teacher's approval. If we dress the way others dress, listen to the music they do, watch the television shows they do and go to the church they do, we can also avoid risking the loss of their approval. Our fear can therefore prevent us from simply being who we are. Watch how you behave with others. Where does your fear arise?

The warrior feels his fear and accepts it. In England I visited the field where the Battle of Hastings was fought in 1066. This was a turning point in Anglo Saxon history. We could try to remember how these warriors would have felt. A damp morning. The armor is cold on our skin. We hold our swords and peer into the mist across the valley. A raven croaks. Fear arises, along with the damp and the cold, and along with our courage and determination. Our fear tells us both that we are alive, and that soon we will be dead.

Fear of battle is an old one, and may not be the worst by any means. That sort of fear is clean and crisp, and the feel of our armor, the flapping of the pennants, the smell of the horses, and the sight of our friends and foes can sustain us through the endless hours of battle. This is still true today, although the battlefield may have changed. It may be a struggle in the inner city to get proper funding for a local school. It may be the struggle to pay the mortgage on a family farm. It may be in the courtroom where you are arrayed to protect a river from pollution. Or at a political meeting where you stand and speak you mind. Or when you speak into a microphone on national radio. At such moments the momentum of the situation is great enough that fear can be ridden.

The greatest fear is when we are alone, and there is no array of battle to be seen, no comrades to even bury us when we fall. To put on clean clothes even though we live in a slum. To clean up and paint our apartment even though it is only rented. To plant trees when we know the next landowner may cut them all down. To sow a crop again when it has been destroyed by drought the last three years. To write a book which no one may read. To live another day when there seems to be nothing to live for. To wash the dishes and sweep the floors when we know no one will visit. Hear the voice of fear that whispers that there is nothing to live for next week, let alone next year...the fear that one does not exist, and worse still, the fear that one does exist but that it does not make any difference to anyone or anything.

When you see this fear, take a long, hard, careful look at it. Taste it if you can. Feel its texture. Smell it. This is what drives people to madness, drugs, suicide, and mutual self-destruction. In their headlong rush away from it, this is what impels them to write books, build business empires, rob their partners, have multiple lovers, inflict pain, start wars, write plays—anything to prove to themselves that the fear does not exist. Anything to have something to throw at the monster when it next appears.

This monster cannot be driven away even if you attack it with a new lover, a Nobel Prize or a business empire. Neither can a monster like this be truly tamed because it is beyond the realm of friendship. Watch for the parts of your life that bring this monster to the door of the cave. Perhaps with time you may tame him to the point where he can be ridden. Ride him with joy, but never turn your back.

Basic Instructions

Steadfastness
Simplicity
Accommodation
Gentleness
Duty
Stewardship

•••

Steadfastness

The thin red line of British soldiers on a foreign hillside; they do not break and flee even as they face odds of fifty to one and feel the cartridges running low.

Another day on the factory floor, another day's pay. Leaving the parking lot we notice that there are fewer cars there these days. Who will be next?

Another day mopping floors and cleaning toilets in the bus station. Doing a job that everyone needs but few respect. There are no chances for escape; even if you do, someone else must still get the cigarette butts out of the urinals each night.

An ordinary human sitting on a meditation cushion, holding his posture until the gong is rung.

The British paratroopers surrounded at the Arnhem bridge, one bridge too far; hold until relieved. No relief in sight. Waiting for supplies that are dropped instead on the enemy's lines.

There are those times when every part of our body demands action—flight, retreat, advance, attack, regroup—anything but holding. But if the thin red line of steadfastness could build a British Empire upon which the sun never set, then there is something to be learned about holding ground resolutely.

Where in this chaotic, darkening world can we find steadfastness? Not on the television which demands instant action to fulfill our desires; "call the toll free line, have your credit card ready." Not on the VCR where we lure ourselves into believing that problems can be solved in a few hours, where nation states are born, and love affairs resolved in a convenient evening on the sofa. Not in the newspapers, where background fades to insignificance, obscured by the surge of irrelevant detail. Perhaps not even in friends who fall away as our circumstances decline. We will have to seek it out and find it where we can. How will we recognize it?

Being steadfast means that we can feel the earth beneath our feet and the sky overhead. There is the practicality of earth, mixed with the vision of sky. If we feel panic gaining the upper hand, he can take courage from a good sergeant. Meanwhile, up and down, hope and fear, good and bad, live and die, have and lose, black and white—our ordinary minds beat back and forth like pistons. Keep the clutch in. Wait.

We can stand like flagpoles. Chogyam Trungpa Rinpoche often spoke of posture in this way. We are rooted in the ground. We are steadfast. We hold our place. Displays of phenomena arise around us. Clouds pass overhead. Thoughts flutter like flags in a stiff breeze, or else hang languidly in thick, steamy air. Just thoughts. Just phenomena. Wait.

We must not confuse steadfastness with mere stubbornness. Stubbornness is blind. It acts out of instinct. Out of fear. Out of clinging. Out of jealousy. Out of ignorance. The parent who mis-treats his child because what was good enough for him must be good enough for his offspring. The supervisor broken by the sys-tem who can see no choice but to stick to worn-out plans that did not work twenty years ago and will not work now, who blocks younger people he could help, the anti-mentor. The fearful fun-damentalist denying a century of scientific progress. The injured friend who has fallen, urging us not to go bravely on, but to weaken and accept defeat. These are not steadfast comrades, nor are they brave sergeants we can trust. They would have us con-fuse cowering with bravery under fire.

How can we tell steadfastness from stubbornness as each aris-es? Steadfastness has space and vision and heart. Space. We know where we are. We can see the terrain. We can feel the movement in the field around us. Fear, irritation, panic, pain, revulsion, desire, these all arise—and yet still we stand our ground. There is vision too. We have plans and the sky above. There is a natural logic to it all; if we break our line and run we will be hunted down and speared one by one. Only by holding to our line will we survive.

Yet steadfastness draws upon much more than mere logic—we must hear the voices that tell us to run, acknowledge them, and rouse the courage of earth and vision of sky to stay. It is the nat-ural expression of our earth nature combined with our sky nature. Earth without sky has a sense of stubbornness; therefore add vision and stir.

Steadfastness also has a sense of heart. It is a popular theme today to accuse men of being out of touch with our hearts and our feelings. When we are steadfast, we can feel the beating of our heart, smell the fear and pain of others. The more we stay steady, the more our heart can expand, the more we can feel the sadness of human circumstances—we could feel the wind blowing through our ribs and rushing across our heart, yet still stand.

If we cannot feel space, vision or heart in our steadfastness, it is time to look around. Are we being steadfast, or stubborn? Only we can tell. Lesser beings who cannot recognize principle or vision will try to confuse us. Therefore we must keep our minds clear and our hearts open.

Steadfastness has two purposes at least. On the outer path, steadfastness is necessary for human beings to accomplish their aspirations. It provides a firm foundation for gripping the phenomenal world. Steadfastness provides a reliable foundation for working with the pain and confusion of other beings. Steadfastness is equally necessary on the inner path of warriorship. Without it, we wander from one spiritual trip to another, life as a flea market, wearing other people's cast-offs, maybe something better will show up tomorrow, no need to risk commitment.

Steadfastness brings each human face to face with the hungry ghosts. Ghosts in the twentieth century? "Do you believe in ghosts, daddy?" my sons used to ask. Look for yourself. Hungry ghosts must first be seen clearly in all their seductive guises before they can be put to rest. This is one reason why we meditate. Listen for the ghostly voices which invent excuse after excuse, ploy after ploy, to get us to leave our ranks, abandon our cushion. A baloney sandwich never seemed so inviting. A cup of tea. A piece of fruit. Some fresh air. The bathroom. To stand and stretch one's back. To write that long-delayed letter. To look out the window. This is the way a coward lives life, drawn from one instant to another by craving, irritation, flickering thoughts of desire, the endless search for fulfillment. We are all haunted by the hungry ghosts, huge empty bellies with pinhole mouths, sucking, craving, following, aching, wanting, seeking, grasp-ing—creating delusion and pain. Hungry ghosts are all around us once we start to look for them—in our office, beside us on the bus, hanging out in the halls, buying in the malls, collecting at the flea market, feeding in the restaurants.

Steadfastness provides a cool breaking dawn, pale blue sky with orange streaks, Venus shimmering, a dawn that gradually banishes these hungry ghosts.

Shield your energy. Watch for distractions. Pick your fights. Do not give in to fear and irritation. Take your place in the world. Hold until relieved.

Simplicity

Simplicity is a virtue in this dark age.

*L*ittle boys collect things. Rocks with strange colors, white rocks, black rocks, acorn caps, leaves, twigs, coins, baseball cards, partly chewed gum with some flavor left, feathers, string, elastic bands—my sons' jacket pockets were so full that often there was no room for hands. Each day they would come up the driveway with more precious stones to add to their collection. I do not know if they noticed, but while each one was a fine specimen on its own, each also shrank back to just a stone again when added to the growing pile in the plastic bucket.

Big boys collect things too. Televisions, CD players, CDs, books, plants, furniture, bank accounts, stocks, mortgages, degrees, expectations, hopes, fears, shoes, suites, tools, dishes, cars… The more things we have, the more there are to lose. The more we have, the more there are to break. The more we have, the more it costs to fix them. The more we have, the more we want anyway. Many possessions cause more pain than they are worth. Therefore, exercise restraint. Practice simplicity.

A cluttered environment creates clutter for the mind. Perhaps we could have fewer pictures on the wall, fewer ornaments on the table, one less piece of furniture in the room. This is our home; it is not a museum, nor is it a garage sale. Sometimes we are so intimidated by space that we actually try to fill it. Reverse the process. Give yourself some space to breathe. Repeatedly practice this warrior art of making space. If it takes a while to get up the courage, start with the closet and get rid of the clothes that you haven't worn for two years. Why hold onto that badly fitting shirt anyway?

Often our mind is the same as our home, or our closet. How many stories, memories, notions, beliefs, hopes and fears are cluttering up the space. Let them go! Have a mental garage sale! Maybe if we moved away some of the mental obstacles, there would be space. Space for a fresh breeze of delight. Space for us to dance. Space for something new to come for a visit.

At the same time that we are making space, we could be cautious. We have to carefully discriminate between simplicity and self-denial. The former is a virtue that liberates, whereas the latter just generates inner turmoil. Self-denial can simply reflect self-hatred or a feeling of worthlessness. When we talk about simplicity, we are not talking about burning the furniture and sleeping on the floor, nor emptying the closets and wearing a burlap bag. The space can still accommodate a fine, comfortable, black leather chair; the closet needs that beautiful hand-embroidered blouse that brings out the green in your eyes. We can simplify and yet be gentle with ourselves at the same time. In fact, we can enrich the space by making it elegant. The Buddha himself spent many years in strict self-denial, erroneously believing that it would bring enlightenment. But it was only when he ate a little food, and took a comfortable seat in the shade, that his mind opened.

I once read a whole book on the virtues of voluntary simplicity. After the first 150 pages, it appeared that the author had missed his own point. Let me not make the same mistake here.

Simplicity is the antidote to this dark age of consumerism and confusion, the antidote that releases one from the grasp of craving, confusion and self-denial.

Practice simplicity. Make some space at home. Enliven it with just enough elegance to make guests feel welcome.

Accommodation

There are many fools in the world. Part of our practice is learning to recognize them. Trust yourself to know when you are right, and stand up for things you believe in. In general, we probably conform to our circumstances more than we need to. We could resist more conformity. But as we resist conformity, we must understand the benefits of accommodation.

Accommodation is far more of an art than we might first think. It is therefore easily overlooked in our lives. Accommodation is one of many subtleties that allow us to work skillfully with other people. Let us consider the nuances of accommodation, acceptance, and acquiescence.

Acquiescence has the sense of giving in to others against our better judgment. It has connotations of reluctance, or resistance, of negativity. We acquiesce if we have been overwhelmed or worn down. Some people will try to wear us out just so we become exhausted to the point where we can only acquiesce. This is a truly despicable tactic because such people are concerned neither with the merits of ideas, nor with our physical or mental health. They care for nothing except getting their own way. If we discover this is being done, it is a rare opportunity—take a good look because here is a glimpse of evil at work in the world. We can avoid such people as if they were homicidal maniacs. If we want to see this sort of mind at work from a safe distance, we could watch *Silence of the Lambs*. Accommodation is not acquiescence. Accommodation comes from a sense of power, not a sense of defeat.

Acceptance is somewhat less negative. It implies a general air of neutrality about things as they are. Acceptance does not have the tone of reluctance that acquiescence has. There is considerable wisdom in accepting those circumstances that we cannot change. But if we look at history, we often find it all too easy to acquiesce to, or accept, circumstances that can actually be changed for the better. If there is a hidden weakness at the core of philosophies which preach acceptance, such as Buddhism, it lies in this tendency to accept injustice and reinforce fatalism. A great deal of human suffering has been eradicated with simple steps such as clean drinking water, sewers, schools, improved crops, and antibiotics.

Both acquiescence and acceptance describe stances we could take to situations which appear to be beyond our control. Accommodation is neither of these. If we are working with others skillfully, we could be feeling not so much acquiescence or acceptance as joy. Accommodating others can mean seeing the wisdom in their vision, and joining in for a while for the sheer pleasure of companionship. Or there can be mutual accommodation as we discover the joy of collaborating to accomplish a shared vision. Our joy in accommodation may go back to hunter-gatherer days when we would follow an elder, skilled in hunting, for days to find food. No doubt there were times when this may have been done with a sense of acquiescence or acceptance, particularly if there were doubts about the elder's hunting skills, but we can imagine it often had the joy of companionship and shared goals.

The energy of accommodation is the raw material for the actual creation of human society. It is the campfire, and the food, and the dancing. This energy can be thought of as one of the qualities which anger can protect; anger could be the protector at the edge of the gathering. A society with no protectors will surely perish, but those who forget what they are protecting ultimately die as well. A person, a camp and a society need a heart of accommodation.

When they see accommodation from a distance, some cynics may observe that it is not so much what you know as who you know. If we find ourselves making this observation, we may need to take a second look. Perhaps they are all accommodating one another, and it is time to join the party.

Gentleness

"Blessed are the meek: for they shall inherit the earth."
(Matthew 5:5)

*S*hall they? Now here is something to question. How could it possibly be true? Did the meek ever get their civil rights, were they ever freed from their bondage? I see no evidence for it. From Spartacus to John Brown, from Wat Tyler to Joe Hill, men have had to act to escape oppression and inherit their piece of earth.

Yet we are told that we should cultivate meekness, and not only that, but gentleness and mercy, too.

How could anyone suggest and commend these in this dark age of "take no prisoners"; surely we have to toughen ourselves up in tough times? Yet we know too, perhaps it is our voice of enlightenment, that the world is crying out for exactly such qualities; the world needs compassion. How is it that such a contradiction occurs?

My parental fear of recommending these qualities lies in this observation: when we see people exercising meekness, it frequently has an unnerving edge about it. So often it seems that they are meek because they feel themselves to be powerless; they have decided that it is better to adapt to being a slave than to live like a free human. Perhaps they are meek because their spirit is broken, merciful only because they are afraid to assert themselves, virtuous only because they are scared of what others might say, and modest only because they have nothing to say. I would not want my own sons among such people, and cannot suggest that this kind of meekness is enlightened behavior in any form.

Perhaps, though, this is not really what is meant by being meek. Are we really being advised to just let others wash the floor with us? We might dismiss the one quote as being only relevant to Roman times, as being just for some Christians, as being a mis-translation, as being somehow wrong. But then we encounter Buddhist teachers who say the same thing with nearly identical words, using words such as 'gentleness.' In fact, Chogyam Trungpa Rinpoche used to shock people by telling them the fundamental quality of a warrior was meekness. What could teachers like these be getting at? It would appear that we have somehow forgotten whatever wisdom might arise out of gentleness, meekness and mercy. Perhaps we can no longer even identify the circumstances where they are appropriate. Moreover, even if we did wish to express them in our lives, lacking good examples, we have no idea how to begin. We may be like a painter who has never seen the colour blue and has no idea where to find it, how to mix it on the palette or how to put it in a painting. We may thereby be diminished, blinded, crippled.

Here is where we might wish to consider the king principle, both literally, and as a particular kind of energy which can arise in our lives. A monarch could afford to be modest, virtuous,

merciful and gentle precisely because he had the power and confidence to do so. These traits arise out of power and confidence.
This appears to be the point. A king without mercy is a tyrant. A
human being without mercy, then, is just a smaller tyrant.

We could imagine experiencing this king principle in our
lives. We could envision humans who are gentle because they
are confident in themselves and their ideas; they have no need to
advance their ideas sharply. They are gentle because they can let
the situation speak for itself. They are modest because they are
living out their own life of power, following a path, and so have
no coward inside who cries out to be noticed and complimented.
Their many virtues arise not out of fear of what others will say,
not out of self denial, not out of fear of heaven or hell, but
because virtue is their way of being. They stand on the earth
solidly; they feel the sky above and remain steadfast on the earth
below. They are merciful because they appreciate the pain and
confusion in other's lives. They are gentle with others because
they have learned to be gentle with themselves. When we
describe 'meek' in this way, we can appreciate how we might
express the quality of gentleness without compromising ourselves.

To discover this confident gentleness in ourselves, we may
have to search for parts of ourselves we discarded long ago.
When many of us are growing up, the least sign of gentleness is
ruthlessly attacked. An act of compassion for a friend being bul-
lied, a tear of sadness for a fellow child, the actual raw feeling of
one's own beating heart…these may have been greeted by
resounding cries of "Sissy! Sissy!" Before long, we learn to hate
those parts of ourselves that could open us to such abuse. Where
in our childhood world were examples of gentleness that we
could respect?

Some months ago a video store showed a drill sergeant pushing a recruit's head into a toilet; my two sons laughed at the spectacle and wanted to rent it. I was struck by the simple-minded brutality of it. This was tyrant energy, not king energy. It could only be funny if you were closed to the sadness. Perhaps too many of us have already learned that when we see sad acts, we dare not let ourselves feel that sadness. Perhaps we are afraid that the sadness will be met again with cries of "Sissy!" The coward is afraid to feel sadness because of this very vulnerability. But we might relax and accept the feeling of sadness as it arises.

We may be born with different amounts of inherent sadness and mercy, just as our arms and our bodies are different sizes and shapes. Yet, too often it seems that we cannot respect this quality in ourselves, in others, or in our children. Because we do not understand true gentleness, because we confuse gentleness with cowardice, we try to destroy it. "Toughen them up so they can survive as men," is what my great-grandfather would probably have said about children, particularly sons. Our challenge may be instead to find a way to protect the world from angry tyrants, and to create more merciful kings. As parents we could try to protect this quality of mercy, we could help our children carry it forward into adulthood, we could guide them in expressing this quality to the world. As an adult, we could respect the gentleness in ourselves and in those around us. The point seems to be that we can be steadfast, and strong, and take our places in the world without losing our hearts in the process.

The world is a sad place. And that can be a very natural source of our gentleness. Even as we draw our sword, we could feel sadness for the unfortunate soldiers of the tyrant who will die that day. Without the sadness, we are no different from the tyrant we seek to overthrow. But that does not mean that we have to sit down and cry. We could draw our sword and cry out for justice, yet feel compassionate tears in our eyes as we do. The tyrant may be only an overbearing in-law, or a cruel co-worker, or a rude customer. Tyrants come in all shapes and sizes. We could feel our gentleness and mercy even as we use the sharp point of our sword to gently wake them up to their responsibilities as fellow human beings. We don't have to chop off their heads and put them up for display on posts. We need not slaughter them without quarter. We could mercifully wake them up with a smile. Perhaps the gentle touch of a sword on their neck might wake them up to their own confusion or aggression. We could try saying "Enough is enough!" without following through with a sword in the belly. Instead of trying to rip it out, we could reach in and lightly touch their heart. We could study the terrain in order to find the right way to be gentle and firm, meek and courageous, merciful and determined.

Practice the true heart of gentleness. Do not let others shove you around as you do.

Duty

Let us turn to a hard truth of adulthood and maturity: duty and virtue. Without these attributes, we remain perpetually a child. A twelve-year-old boy is fine; a thirty-year-old boy is a tragedy. One of the characteristics of these dark times is the failure of boys to become men, the failure of girls to become women. There is a decline in respect for knowledge and wisdom, and there is a lack of concern for one's duties and responsibilities to society. Cowards prefer emasculation and weakness. Cowards use hard times as their excuse for evading responsibility.

Duty does not, however, need to be particularly heavy-handed. Being an adult means that we get to drive a real piece of heavy equipment instead of pushing a toy through the sand box. Even meditation retreats usually have several hours of manual duties daily. Our urge to hide out and stay a child seems to be a manifestation of fear. We really would like to keep our little lips on the nipple and a diaper conveniently in place; in contrast, chewing our own food, walking down the hall to the toilet, it all seems like just too much effort.

We could equally have the mistaken view that duty is just a way of punishing ourselves. We may imagine that just because we are doing something we think is debasing, it must have merit. Maybe we think that cleaning the toilets in a monastery would be a fine way of proving our humility, of showing the world that they we are truly working at spirituality. Perhaps we will have to keep it up until we realize that cleaning the toilet at home, or paying taxes, or voting, has just as much—and just as little—virtue. We could just keep it simple. In the Zen tradition, working as a cook is highly regarded. A good Zen cook keeps the kitchen clean. If nothing else, cleanliness protects the monks from food poisoning. Keeping the kitchen clean is just another example of responsibility. We keep the kitchen clean in a monastery for the same reason that we drive on the right side of the road—things work out better because of this discipline.

We can seek out some middle way between staying a baby in our diaper and taking duty to self-hating extremes. But as we practice finding the balance, duty still calls. In fact, as some people remain child-like and abandon their responsibilities to society, other adults must be prepared to take their places. As cowards abandon the thin red line, we must fill the gaps. As raw recruits are increasingly thrust into positions of power, we must train them. As the arenas fill up across the continent, as human minds turn to monster trucks, bingo, baseball and hockey, others must gird themselves with the practices of duty, responsibility and virtue.

What exactly does responsibility entail? In one sense, words like duty and virtue echo back thousands of years in western history. Our knowledge of civilization and of the great ideas that it produced appears to be waning; the situation may well get even worse. Yet classical ideas like virtue and duty have influenced our civilization for millennia. Ancient writers can speak to us today—Sophocles, Aristophanes, Aristotle; Virgil, Plutarch, Tacitus; Descartes, Swift, Voltaire; how many of these do we now read in school? As we forget them, we end up with a form of social Alzheimer's disease, an obsession with the ephemera of the present, a collective decerebration, a slow lobotomizing of our culture.

At the ordinary practical level, the most basic adult virtues are simple passive ones—pay your taxes, obey the law. These are quite straightforward and simple. It is surprising how many of us do not want to grow up and accept this. Somehow we want to believe that if we elude the state, or cheat other people, we must be clever. Perhaps we keep a few more dollars in our wallet, but what is clever about keeping a child's mind? Perhaps part of the problem is that we believe that we are cheating someone anonymous out there; we fail to see that we are stunting ourselves as surely as if we drank poison. Or, we may decide to evade our duties by going on what seems like an exotic spiritual adventure, say to Thailand. We may be shocked to find that we still have to sit still on a cushion until the gong is rung, help in the kitchen preparing supper, or clean the cooking pots.

Of course, the practice of duty does not call for unthinking obedience. Duty can entail refusing to obey. It is tempting to dwell on the heroic exceptions, to pump ourselves up and imagine all the times when we must break the rules for higher moral reasons. But before we get side-tracked, it is important to remind ourselves of the rarity of such circumstances. Being on this path means that we begin to accept and appreciate the ordinary world for what it is. Not every night has magnificent rainbows, nor tornadoes for that matter. Most of the time we must obey the law. Period. We drive on the right side of the road, we stop at stop signs, we pay our bills, we mail in our taxes, we clean the bathroom, we sit in the meditation hall when the gong rings, we attend to the basic details of our lives.

Yet there may be times when duty requires us to disobey unjust rules. This is not some trendy new idea. Long before Christianity, the Greek playwright Sophocles wrote about conflict between civic laws and moral laws. In the play *Antigone*, written around 440 BC, King Creon has decreed that the corpse of a young man cannot be buried, but must be left to rot. Antigone buries her brother anyway. She is brought before King Creon who asks how she could break his laws. She replies, "I did not think that the orders of a mere mortal man could overrule the laws of the gods." And so a tragedy unfolds, for King Creon is determined to uphold his civil laws, just as Antigone insists upon adherence to moral laws.

The other day a youth sailed past me through a red light on a skate board. He broke the law without a second thought. Both Antigone and Gandhi would probably have been as irritated as I was. Obey the laws if you possibly can; social order is based upon this. If you believe you must break the law, do not do it mindlessly on a skate board. Know you act from virtue, try to repeal the law if you can; as a last resort be prepared to join the ranks of Antigone and Gandhi.

Participation is a second civic virtue. It provides a means to change laws we don't like. The world is full of whiners and complainers. If you interrupt the complainers to ask them if they voted, and for whom, one frequently finds that they have not participated in even this most elementary act of citizenship, or that they voted for the very political party they are bitterly complaining about. Of course it is always easier to complain about our mummy and daddy than to grow up and run our own household, or our own country.

How does an adult make real positive changes in an imperfect world? How do we avoid falling into cheap formulas, narrow mindedness, cynicism or intolerance? A period on a meditation cushion, or in a Zen monastery, may be a wise use of one's time. But the only way to tell if we learned anything at all is to get up and work with the real world as it is—whether this requires us to change diapers or stand to speak in the legislature.

The ultimate act of participation is to seek office for oneself. It is one thing to sweep the corrupt from power; it is another to heal the wounds they created; and it is quite another again to apply the necessary combination of vision and skill to build a more enlightened society. But if we do not step into the breach to exercise power for the benefit of society, that breach will be filled by those confused souls who are attracted by power without purpose.

To seek public office at this time is to be tarred with the same brush as scoundrels. How much easier it would be to crack open a beer and snooze in front of the latest football game on the television. How much more acceptable it would be to buy seasons tickets for the local team at the local arena and fill in the evenings with beer, hot dogs and cheering for men with different colored shirts. How much more peaceful it would be to buy a membership in the local golf club and spend our days on the greens with friends. How much easier it may be to remain a child.

If we find ourselves deterred by the behavior of scoundrels and liars, we can remember that we are needed all the more: tyrants are born out of cynicism and public lethargy. We need leaders to serve so that dangerous men do not rise to fill the vacuum. But rather than acting out of duty, perhaps we could inspire ourselves with evocations of other men of service: Tyler, Huss, Cromwell, Voltaire, Pitt, Danton, Hill, Sandino, Gandhi, Roosevelt, Churchill,

Douglas, Kennedy, Pearson, Dayan, Brown, Dubcek, Havel. How many of these names do we now recognize? The world needed people such as these. Why not join them?

When an ancient city state was surrounded by a foreign army, duty was clear for all to see. Who would accept the risks of battle, and who would hide in bed with a concubine or try to profiteer? The rest of the city would be watching in the streets, or from the walls. If there is a difference between then and now, it is that a foreign army at the gates poses a threat obvious to even the criminally stupid. Recognizing and addressing problems such as inequality of wealth, ozone holes and overpopulation requires somewhat more sophistication. Yet at least in the Greek cities there were playwrights and poets who spoke out loudly for virtue and duty. I lack their eloquence, but feel that I have now done my small part in their great tradition.

Finally, the cost of duty should not be overestimated. We have more allies than we often realize. The service of others can be a source of joy and confidence. Much of our current despondency and fear may be because our self-centered lives now cut us off from both the joy of service and the confidence of achievement. Let me be very clear on this point: our lives attract the sort of energy we habitually use. If we seek the benefit of others through a life of service and heroism, we may find these energies rising from nowhere (and everywhere) to serve beside us. Heroes attract the energy that they need to live their lives; in a like manner, cowards attract cowardice and other cowards.

As we take up our responsibilities, mixing duty with joy becomes a constant challenge. Joy may at first seem somehow opposed to duty. Perhaps it is partly the fear of losing joy that seduces us to hang out, to avoid responsibility, and to seek a life that only has pleasure. Even as we take this route, it does not seem to work for long. Like some sort of pendulum, joy and duty change back and forth from moment to moment. Activities that start out as joy rapidly become a duty—an article written in joy becomes duty when proofs arrive for correction; a child conceived in joy needs its diapers changed; a new car still needs to be washed. Moreover, it seems that if we strive for joy alone, some sort of balance is disrupted, and we actually generate more suffering for ourselves. The joy of cutting firewood may be disrupted because we avoided our duty to maintain the tractor. This leads to the added frustration of being stranded in the woods, having to walk out and call a neighbor to drive us back. Similarly, the joy of owning a house and entertaining may, if we ignore our duties, quickly give way to the frustration of living with a leaky roof or clogged pipes.

Perhaps we could think of life as a kind of stew. There are lumps of parsnip and turnip—the duties of life. And there are lumps of meat—the joys of life. We need both to make a tasty and satisfying stew. If we try to cheat by only eating the meat, or punish ourselves by only eating the turnips, we miss something. The fact is that the meat makes wonderful sauce for the parsnips and turnips, and they in turn add a depth and texture to the meat. Only children make piles of the parsnips and turnips on the sides of their plates.

Duty and responsibility are virtues of adulthood. Accepting them marks our coming of age. Do not give in to the lemming-like rush to cowardice and decerebration. Duty. Responsibility. Steadfastness. Service. Adulthood.

Stewardship

"But this I say, He which soweth sparingly shall
reap also sparingly; and he which soweth
bountifully also shall reap bountifully."

II Corinthians 9:6

et me introduce a word that already sounds archaic—
stewardship. We are all stewards because we only live a short
time and pass our world on to others. Yet throughout history,
barbarians on horseback have swept down out of the hills,
burned the cities, and carried off the work of farmers and arti-
sans. Unable to create for themselves, barbarians are reduced to
mere pillage. A steward is different. A steward cultivates; he
gradually improves the farm he manages. He certainly does not
pillage it. Farmers practice stewardship when they look after
their soil and buildings, and leave their sons and grandsons a
legacy. Each other occupation, from business owner to teacher,
however, has its own kind of stewardship.

This could be a time for despair. Perhaps that explains the fading of the word stewardship. It sometimes appears that it is
dying even among our farmers. In the rural community around

me, neighbors are mining the soil to sell to the city, over-cutting their forests, splitting off lots for rural sprawl, and voting for conservative politicians who are eagerly abandoning the laws and regulations that protect the rural environment. In their greed and their profligacy with our planet, they appear to have forgotten that conservative and conservation have the same root. In short, they are behaving in a way that will destroy their own way of life, and it is happening so quickly that one cannot now drive to the city without seeing new destruction daily.

But we need not despair, because stewardship is an inherent quality of human beings. How else did we create great civilizations but by sowing, harvesting and sharing? How many generations of courageous farmers are already stored in our genes and flowing in our arteries? We can practice stewardship wherever we live. We can leave the office in better shape than when we moved in. We can leave our house in better repair than when we bought it. We can leave our friends in better situations for having known us. We can leave our forest with more big trees than we started with. We can leave our city in a better shape by running for public office.

We particularly need this quality of stewardship in public office, be it municipal, provincial, state or national politics. In spite of what cynics seem anxious to make us believe, most humans have a genuine understanding of stewardship, and most are prepared to sacrifice for this ideal. Humans *do* naturally want to leave a better world for their offspring. Many times it seems that our elected representatives will not give us the option of stewardship. It sometimes seems as if they cannot believe that humans could care for their land and their children.

Here is where each of us could begin to trust ourselves. We could actually feel that stewardship is part of our inheritance. Perhaps we have let it become overgrown by our greed, our fear, our lack of trust. One way to avoid these destructive agents is to reconnect with the power of cultivation wherever it arises. We can learn to recognize soil and potential for cultivation wherever it may be found. We can start this practice here and now. We can look for opportunities to give instead of take. We can do it until it becomes an enlightened habit.

It takes the most courage to sow when we do not know whether we will be there to harvest. This is often our life. It sometimes seems that it just is not worth the effort to try again. The point seems to be that if we sow enough seeds, some will survive until the harvest. This is just basic applied biology. If we are miserly and hoard our seeds, however, we may indeed find that none survive. The miser simply proves to himself that the world is miserly.

We, in contrast with the miser, could sow at least one seed every day, wherever we are. Help a friend with a problem. Teach a student. Write an article for the newspaper. Donate money to a charity. Fix something for someone else. Thank someone for their help. Each of these is a seed. Each might grow into something magnificent. Of course, it might also wither in the summer sun or freeze in an early frost. We do not know. But if we allow our fear to overwhelm us, we end up with no seeds in the ground at all.

We may even believe that we will be better off to eat the few seeds we have rather than consign them to the ground. We can daily see people around us eating their own seeds, and then wondering why they are hungry.

A warrior knows that we must protect the land and allow cultivation to occur. The risky act of sowing seeds is the only way to get a harvest. Still afraid to sow? We may gain courage from stories throughout history of villagers who have endured death by starvation rather than eat the seeds they had put aside for the next harvest. If they could stand such deprivation in order to trust their seed to a future harvest, what excuse do we have for having less confidence than them? A life of sowing seeds, even strange ones we do not recognize, is bound to leave a harvest to enjoy in later life. Perhaps when faced with difficult decisions, we could ask ourselves this question: which actions will make me most satisfied when I look back on them from the age of eighty? If we actually picture ourselves on the front porch of a retirement home, we can ask which path of action will we regret, and which will make us proud?

The Bible tells us explicitly that we shall end up harvesting in proportion to what we have sown. Buddhists agree; they explain further that every act not only sows a seed in the external world, but it also sows a seed in our own minds. An act of selfishness sows a seed for further grasping and pain in our lives; an act of stewardship sows a seed for future happiness and harvest. This is part of the process of karma. We need not concern ourselves here with the consequences of sowing bad deeds or bad seeds, because we will aspire to right attitude; we do not want to be motivated by fear. Of course, we may sow the occasional weed by mistake, but as long as we have right intention, as long as we feel an enlightened attitude, these mistakes will be few and far between.

The world can have the qualities of both a wasteland and a garden. It may look desolate during a drought, it may seem that we will never pass that way again. When we fall despondent, we could recall the words of President John Kennedy: "Ask not what your country can do for you; ask what you can do for your country." We can ask with our heart and mind, we can listen to the answer, we can act, we can act even if it seems outrageous.

Be a steward. Commit random, outrageous acts of generosity. Inspire others to do the same.

Experiences Arise

Joy
Anger
Shame
Aloneness
Ignorance
Revulsion
Naiveté

•••

Joy

Why is it that humans can feel joy? From the point of view of human biology, joy may simply indicate that we are living life fully. Joy is like the gauge that tells us our oil pressure is sufficient to protect the car's engine. The experience of joy is a way for us to be told by our brains and bodies that all is well. After all, falling in love, having sex, and raising children, all bring joy. This is no accident. If these were unpleasant, human beings would have ceased reproducing and died out long ago.

Similarly, collecting food, cooking a fine meal and sharing it with friends also brings joy. We are social beings. If we did not take pleasure in each other's company, we probably would also have died out long ago. Eating collectively is a wonderful activity because it nourishes our individual physical needs at the same time as our social needs.

We could trust this kind of joy. It is like trusting in the basic sanity of life, the basic decency of human existence. There is a tendency today to feel guilt when we feel joy. Often there appears to be a rule that warns that what we are doing is against divine law, or society's will, or our doctor's advice, or at least is vaguely bad for us somehow. Even if we escape these sources of guilt, we can always ask whether it is fair for us to feel joy when others are clearly suffering. But we can see the two are quite unconnected. Whether or not we feel joy has no connection to whether or not others are suffering. Who knows, perhaps if we were acting in a way that created more joy in our lives, others might be suffering less. Perhaps it is infectious.

We might confuse joy with the mere absence of discomfort. Or we might use the search for pleasure to hide out. We might find ourselves trying to create a cozy little nest. Or we might try to numb ourselves, preferring dull ignorance to cool clarity. We could even try to intoxicate ourselves with food and drink and revelry just to avoid feeling anything unpleasant. Joy, however, cannot be manipulated so easily. It arises spontaneously. Joy does not fear the unpleasant, nor does it fear reality. Rather, it has a fresh quality of openness and spaciousness, and maybe even sadness. We could know that we are about to die and yet still feel joy.

How do we know if we are doing what we are here for? Perhaps it is doing that which makes us joyful.

Anger

nger is everyone's inheritance. But some of us appear to receive a larger estate than others. It may feel like we inherited a loathsome velvet painting, or an ugly ripped sofa, or a house with termites. We may find it hard to imagine that our inheritance of anger could be appreciated.

Yet anger is only a basic ape instinct. Something threatens us, and we attack. It may be a direct threat to our survival—something, say, like a saber-tooth lion—that gets our ape heart pumping and our muscles tensed. Or it may be a loss—a predator stealing our food, a member of the tribe taking our mate—and we rouse ourselves for the fight to hold on. Anger is as necessary to apes and humans as our eyes, bones or fingers. But it can also blind us, weaken us and destroy us. The challenge is for us to use our anger wisely.

To begin to develop a relationship with anger, we could appreciate that it is just a particular style of energy that arises. In its most basic form, it is like gasoline, neither good nor bad. It may be a gift or it may be a curse, depending upon circumstances, depending upon our skill. Here we may think of the unfortunate woman named Cassandra, the woman for whom the Cassandra complex is named. Cassandra was loved by the god Apollo, and he gave her a beautiful gift, the power of prophecy. When he later regretted giving her the gift, he decreed that although she would have the gift of prophecy, she would never be believed. Thus Cassandra's divine power was simultaneously a beautiful gift and a monstrous curse.

Anger is like this. In its gift form, it is that energy which motivates us to accomplish. Anger is the energy that tells us we don't have to sit back and take it any more. Anger at injustice fueled those who fought to emancipate slaves. Anger at tyranny lead to the American War of Independence and the drafting of what is arguably one of the world's great democratic documents, the American Constitution. Frustration with ignorance and human suffering lead early scholars to reject religious dogma and launch the path of scientific discovery which is still changing the world around us. Anger, then, can be the fuel of human innovation and the source of our courage. Those of us who possess an uncommon amount of anger, are not necessarily cursed. We may have a special role to play in society.

What would happen if we successfully banished anger from our realm? We might be left only with complacency. Complacency, too, is a potential source of evil in the world. Here we are not talking about accommodation, or the enlightened quality of acceptance; we are talking about complacency to the suffering of others. This renders us less than human. Complacency is a kind of ignorance that allows us to ignore what is happening to our neighbor, our co-worker, our tribe, our community, other living creatures and our world. In the 1930s, complacency to the Spanish Civil War arguably made inevitable the success of Nazism in Europe. Complacency has allowed American citizens to support wicked totalitarian regimes in countries such as El Salvador, Guatemala and Chile, countries whose names have become synonymous with the practice of torture. And now complacency lies thick in the air as species disappear forever, as the ozone hole grows, and as our population explodes. A possessor of anger, at least, cannot be complacent.

Anger plays a role not unlike that of camp sentry. Someone has to listen for the approach of danger, warn others and act to protect them. But that does not mean that we have to interrupt the party every time a twig snaps or we see a pair of eyes in the dark. The sentry who sets off the alarm every ten minutes is getting jumpy. Perhaps someone could loan him a meditation cushion. Similarly, the complacent sentry who is asleep on the job is equally a risk to our realm. It may be that the occasional false alarm is far better than suddenly finding our kingdom invaded. The occasional attack might even be welcomed in order to train the guards. We may discover that the complacent sentry also needs the discipline of time alone on a cushion. The world can be calm and quiet, or outrageous and threatening, and we depend upon the sentry to keep our community safe in either case.

Anger does have its dark side. It seems that the sentry too often gets a gun and runs amok and threatens our children and stops the party and annoys our friends. Perhaps this is why we fear it so. Perhaps this is why we try to push it away until we can no longer do so and then it explodes into our world with an undisciplined life of its own. It is no coincidence that the military believes in drill, drill, and more drill before sentries are given a weapon. We instinctively fear this undisciplined power of anger. What we frequently fail to remember is that this anger, in the raw form of unconditioned energy, is neither good nor bad. If we struggle with it, we may only strengthen it. A spiritual path clarifies the activity of anger. It lets us watch the sentries at work.

But as we practice an enlightened relationship with anger, we must continually beware of letting it harm others. Working with anger does not mean that we can dump it out on the floor of the office and leave it as a mess for other people to clean up. This is not just poor practice on the path, it is simple bad manners. Moreover, we must avoid intellectual frameworks that seem to legitimize the aggression that arises from anger. The Biblical injunction to spare the rod and spoil the child is a perfect example. How many parents still take out their frustration and anger on their children, confusing their own anger with divine will? A preacher in Ottawa was accused of beating his infant son with a stick; he quoted the Bible in his defense. Imposing our will on another human is not enlightened behavior. Accepting our anger does not mean that we can indulge ourselves at other people's expense.

Anger, though, is a normal ape experience. If you do not feel some anger in your life somewhere, it is time to go out and look for it. A human being without anger is like a human being without skin.

In a quite remarkable way, we may discover, with time, that having anger makes us a protector of the world. Our path, whether we like it or not, requires us to recognize dangers, know what to protect, and how to act skillfully. This may seem like an impossible task. But it takes many years of practice to accomplish any worthwhile goal. It takes a certain degree of steadfastness, patience and determination to learn to play the piano well, to earn a black belt, to learn auto repair, or to skillfully wield a sword. We can start now. We may surprise ourselves. Putting it another way, the anger is already there in the house, just like a grandmother's grand piano in the corner or a grandfather's sword on the wall. Instead of turning our back, or wishing we could put them out for the garage sale, we could brush away the dust and take a second look.

Resist habitual aggression. Practice good manners. Treat anger like a monstrous troll who walks at your side—difficult to approach, a wonderful ally, a possible servant, but never a master.

Shame

We continually meet people who try to shame us into acting the way they want. A person who aspires to be a warrior trains to watch for shame. Unlike the shining broadsword of anger, shame is the knife in the boot, the derringer in the pocket, the bar of soap inside the sock, the poison in the cup of wine.

We could imagine a world where people trusted one another to act decently, a world where we accepted our inherent wisdom as human beings. It is obvious that there are things to be done, and part of living as a human being is doing them. These things could be as basic as cleaning our rooms, washing our bodies and doing the dishes, or as complex as finding a job, running for public office or deciding to have children. But it seems that many people do not trust one another to do what is necessary. We assume others must be shamed into doing what they are supposed to do. If we do not do such and such we are a naughty child, or a troublemaker, or a lazy worker, or a sloppy housekeeper, or a careless teacher...

In a world where shame runs deep, where acts of love are

called sins, and trusting our own hearts is called self-indulgent, we will meet many such shamers. Know them for what they are. Watch for the glint of the hidden weapon. Ultimately we have nothing at all to be ashamed of.

But these are only words. Such advice is as useless as saying, "Watch out for people with automatic weapons and disarm them if they threaten you." It is not that easy! People who rule through shame are very clever at finding that part of our armor where it is weak. Are we secretly afraid that we are not loved by our friends? The shaming friend will see this and say that if we do not try such and such a drug, our friends will desert us. Are we secretly afraid of financial failure? The boss may sense it and imply that if we do not commit a dishonest act, we will be failures. The voice of shame may be most obvious when it is clearly external. But shame cannot work without an ally, without rousing a part of our own self, without depending upon one of our own field commanders being a saboteur.

Therefore, beware of the inner voice of shame. The inner voice of shame, the traitorous commander, can be invoked by someone else, and once this demon has arisen it is inside our own armor; inside our mind, we feel compelled to listen. Afraid that you do not measure up to standards of sexual worth? The voice may tempt you to exploit other beings to demonstrate your prowess to others (and, of course, to yourself). Afraid that you do not matter? The voice will tempt you to climb a mountain or swim a length in a pool faster than other people so that you can get your name written down in a record book. Afraid that you cannot live up to your father's expectations? The voice may challenge you to throw away your inheritance and join the Foreign Legion.

It may help us to recall an incident from the life of the great meditation master, Milarepa, who lived in Tibet about one thou-

sand years ago. Milarepa is renowned for his spontaneous com-
position of poems that reveal the experience of awakened mind.
In this incident, Milarepa is on a long retreat in a cave where he
meditates alone. His practice, *mahamudra*, is to experience the
nature of his own mind as it is; in this practice, any attempts to
reform the mind are regarded as counterproductive. As he practices, he hears a noise at the back of the cave, and finds it is
occupied by a demoness named Draugsrinmo. He debates with
her, and finally subdues her. She then becomes his ally. We may
wonder whether Draugsrinmo was not really a manifestation of
the voice within that says we are worthless, says we are wasting
our time, says we are going nowhere, and weakens us so that
shame can gain control.

Western psychologists, too, such as Bly and Bradshaw,
increasingly warn us just how destructive shame is. They point
out that we all have our own psychological armor which,
metaphorically at least, protects us from other people's moods.
But as children, our moods are easily overrun by dominant
moods from parents. When a parent ignores the child's sover-
eignty, and invades the child, the child can feel ashamed of his
lack of power. A tongue-lashing, a slap across the face, a spank-
ing—all these are weapons which the parent uses to pierce our
armor and penetrate us. If this happens repeatedly, they say, our
inner ally, the one who rises to protect us, is gradually diminished. Every invasion, though it may last only five minutes, can
produce shame which will last decades.

The tragedy in all of this is that it is widely assumed that
shame is necessary to make people act appropriately. It is a most
cynical, degraded view of human beings and human existence.
We do not seem able to trust ourselves, or others, to judge when
things need to be done and then do them. We assume that we

must make someone ashamed of themselves (or, even worse, afraid of God or hell) in order to inspire them to act decently and appropriately. Alas, it may now be partly self-fulfilling. We may be surrounded by people who do not act except to avoid feeling guilt. They do school assignments to avoid guilt. They work to avoid guilt. They visit their parents to avoid guilt. They pay their taxes to avoid guilt. But, in fact, we could do our assignments, work, visit relatives, and pay taxes, all with a sense of joy.

Of course, the flickering of our minds will always invent thousands of additional things we could do. It takes only five seconds for a flicker of thought to tell us that we could visit a sick relative, wash the car, clean the toilet, paint the front porch, call a friend, write a letter, stop a forest from being clear-cut, write a book or practice the piano. Each of these flickers of thought takes only a second to think, but much longer to actually do. So there will always be more flickers of things that may be possible than things that we can actually accomplish in our life. Even as we may be inspired to take on new projects, we cannot let this abundance of things that we might yet do make us feel ashamed of what little we have managed to accomplish. The former must be vastly greater than the latter, just like the Earth must weigh less than the sun. It is Draugsrinmo who would like us to believe otherwise.

Shame is a curse on this period in our civilization. Shame causes mind pollution just the way sewage causes water pollution. Certainly, everything from television commercials to the Catholic church tries to exploit this emotion to control our behavior. A warrior trains to recognize the weapons of his opponents and practices until they can be disarmed without a second thought. Watch for the flicker of shame. Acknowledge the weapon. Then smile and step aside.

Aloneness

Somebody hangs up the telephone and terminates our conversation. Somebody walks out of the room and slams the door. Somebody pulls away when we reach out to touch them. At one instant there was communication, and the next there is space. The sudden sense of aloneness can be remarkably annoying, possibly alarming, even shocking.

We could become very angry. That would be a convenient way to cover up our aloneness. We could call back and then hang up ourselves, or try to slam the door even louder, or buy a book entitled Two Hundred Ways to Get Even. But if we relax with aloneness, we could begin to just feel that experience for what it is. We could perhaps observe that aloneness seems rather akin to fear.

Why are we so afraid of being alone? We might explain it as a natural consequence of the human condition: we don't know where we come from, we don't know what awaits us after death, and companionship in between seems to be the only antidote to complete disorientation. If we were setting out to drive someone mad, we would presumably try to create exactly this situation of knowing neither the beginning, nor the end, nor how long the interim would be. In the film *Blade Runner*, even robots are given childhood memories because it makes them easier to control. Yet, in that same movie, robots too become haunted by not being able to understand their own purpose with no known beginning and an uncertain future.

We might use our logic to observe that our ape mind was groomed to perform in a small tribe. Survival and reproduction depended upon two things: finding a mate, and belonging to the tribe. If one was abandoned by this tribe, one was truly alone. Hunger or predators might then kill us; certainly we would not have a mate. We could therefore say that our minds are programmed to fear isolation from the tribal unit. Our minds are programmed to make us do almost anything to remain a part of the tribal unit. This is accomplished by making us fearful of being alone.

Whatever our logical views on aloneness, it would seem that we need to make a personal, experiential study of this part of our ape instinct. How does it feel? When does it arise? What does it make us want to do? What do we do to avoid it?

We might find, for example, that aloneness makes us feel worthless. If the group does not want us, we must be a bad person. If our mate does not want us, we must be an unworthy man or woman. If our company does not want us, we must be a bad employee. Perhaps we only believe ourselves to be a worthy human being when someone else approves of us. The evolutionary biologist may be able to explain why this instinct would evolve, but that does not necessarily help us live with the experience.

Betrayal may arouse particular bitterness in us because the act of betrayal is a striking declaration: you are alone. When we counted on a member of our tribe, and then find ourselves abandoned to die on the plain with only the vultures as witness, we experience the sharp edge of aloneness. Betrayal gives us no means of escape.

Yet some people have embraced aloneness. Jesus spent forty days and nights in the desert before teaching. Milarepa, the great Tibetan meditation master, spent many years of his life meditating in a cave. The Aboriginal shaman would go alone into the wilderness to encounter the spirit realm. There must, then, be something worthwhile about being alone. Perhaps part of it is that when we are alone, we can see ourselves plainly for what we are. There is no one else's mind messing us up, no one else trying to lay guilt trips on us, no one else slamming down the phone; there is just our mind, starkly silhouetted against a background of rocks and trees.

We may actually be quite shocked to experience our own mind. Perhaps we have been so busy blaming other people for our thoughts and feelings that we are quite astonished to find that these thoughts and feelings arise even when we are alone. Being alone means that there are no excuses. When we have a headache, it seems that the trees and rocks have one too. But if we stay alone, after a while it seems that in some way things begin to calm down. We seem to relate naturally with the trees and the rocks and the space—and our own teacup.

How long do we need to be alone? Jesus fasted forty days and nights in the desert. Buddhists have a traditional thirty-day meditation retreat called a *dathun*. Aloneness, then, can be embraced, but only temporarily. Of course, we could be so afraid of other people that we prefer aloneness to the irritation of other humans.

We could move out to the end of a long dead-end road, we could insult friends when they call for a visit, we could decide it is easier to say home in our cut-offs than to put on a suit and go to a fine restaurant. But even Milarepa, who was, after all, a rather extreme case, eventually left his cave to teach. It would appear that hiding from other people is no way to deal with aloneness.

We could also be so afraid of being alone that we will embrace anything to avoid that feeling. We may marry an obviously unsuitable spouse. We may stay with an abusive mate. We may have children, and more of them. We may hang out with the gang. We may pour ourselves a drink, and then another. We may throw ourselves into the endless party circuit. We may have our evenings at the club, at the card game, in the bingo hall, at the lodge meeting, in the ball park, at the theater. We may start another project. As long as there is activity, as long as other people's minds fill the space around us, we feel secure. Perhaps when we were a small tribe alone on the African plains, there was no choice: we had to stay a part of the tribe, or else we died alone. But now, this urge to keep our lives filled up with friends and acquaintances and just about anyone who is willing to talk to us could be just another expression of fear.

What if we did die alone? We would not be the first. However fearful we may be, many have gone before us on this lonely path. We may drown in a windswept lake. We may slowly freeze in the darkening winter woods. We may find ourselves sleeping on the street and notice that one night the world suddenly grows dim and fades. We may shake a pop machine, only to have it fall and crush us. We may find ourselves in a hospital ward with echoing halls and an IV in our arm. We may be speared and left to die on some foreign hill. Rudyard Kipling once wrote a poem of advice to young British soldiers that goes something like this:

"When you're left wounded on Afghanistan's plains, and the women come out to cut up what remains, just roll to your rifle and blow out your brains, and go to your God like a soldier." Kipling, of course, was most assuredly not advocating routine suicide. But he was acknowledging the fearful truth: even the ultimate team player, the British soldier of the line, might die alone on some foreign hill. If we could just accept this possibility, perhaps it would not cause us so much fear.

It is, of course, natural for humans to build communities, and to want to live and die in them. Our church, our main street, our opera house, our sports team, all of these could provide us with a sense of community. But if they become just a way of hiding from aloneness, it would seem that we are missing the point. Both the socialite and the hermit may be equally driven by fear.

It may be quite natural that some times in life feel crowded: too may kids in the house, too many staff in the office, too many callers at the door. At other times we feel isolated: that sudden click on the telephone, the empty mail box, the deadly silence in hall. Perhaps instead of being panicked, we could take the time to experience the raw situation for what it is. Either way, something is happening. Neither is fundamentally good or bad. We might think about the seasons. Sometimes it is cold, sometimes it is warm. If we spend the winter wishing we could be warm, and the summer wishing we could be cool, then we never really feel either for what it is.

Ignorance

As humans we have an innate desire to be good parents; the urge to care for our young is something we share with all mammals. Yet horrors happen anyway. In China, parents routinely bound up the feet of their daughters so that the foot bones would be crushed and deformed as they grew; the parents crippled their own children believing they were making them more attractive. In some parts of Africa, it is still customary for parents to cut off the genitalia of their daughters, believing that this mutilation will make them more desirable as wives.

Faced with such monstrous acts, we may pride ourselves on what fine parents we all are. Yet, all the same, a monster is eating our children in front of our very eyes. If the monster were a serial killer or a disease, we would be horrified. The monster that is consuming our children, however, is carefully camouflaged; its sneaks in slowly, and then, like some parasitic worm, devours our young from the inside out.

How can such a monster thrive in spite of our best intentions? Part of it may be that the monster does not have a name.

Terminal ignorance is not listed as a source of trouble for children. Ignorance, however, condemns a child to a lifetime of failure and suffering.

Ignorance may at first seem to be just a minor inconvenience; perhaps this is why it manages to hide amongst us. But ignorance is actually the primary cause of human misery. If we do not understand the world around us, if we do not know how it functions, we simply cannot improve our circumstances. Ignorant children are like long-distance drivers who know nothing about car repair, have no spare parts, no extra fuel, and no tool kit—except that the real world has more junkyards than garages. Moreover, the ignorant are perennial victims of the better informed; those who do know how the world works routinely use this knowledge to their own advantage. Ignorance is therefore a direct cause of poverty. This poverty is confounded by confusion, poor communication, poor organization, and all the other routinely frustrating and painful aspects of life. It is surely self-evident that ignorant children cannot look after themselves, even to the simple extent of finding jobs and protecting their health. This sounds depressing perhaps, but it is actually the least of the problems arising out of ignorance.

Even if we should find ourselves in more fortunate conditions, ignorance robs us of the ability to appreciate the pleasures of life. How long will it take us to find out that a house, a car, a bank account and two children will not bring us happiness? It is quite remarkable how many wealthy or well-educated people are still truly miserable. How many marriages end because the couples cannot enjoy life, cannot communicate with one another, and are simply boring one another to death? How many young women still believe that once they have a splashy wedding, life will be perfect thereafter?

Finally, but most importantly, we do not normally understand the full power of ignorance. Ignorance is not just a failure to know certain facts, nor is it just an inability to cope with human life. Ignorance is a destructive mental force that clouds the mind and destroys the ability to appreciate life. Ignorance slowly but inevitably grows from "I don't know" into "I don't want to know." We routinely underestimate the dark power of such ignorance. Ignorance is not like a minor skin rash that will naturally dissipate with time; it is a more like a cancer that grows and deepens, dulling the senses and deadening the mind.

From the Buddhist perspective, ignorance is a powerful mental force that condemns us to endless cycles of frustration and suffering. It actually creates its own claustrophobic little realm, an illusory experience within which we become trapped. Perhaps we fail to protect our children from ignorance because we do not appreciate its destructive power. Ignorance, in fact, feeds upon itself. Ignorance grows with time.

Most parents hope that their children will achieve a least a modest level of material comfort, and then some sort of happiness. Ignorance instead creates the potential for a downward spiral of misery and self-destructiveness. The symptoms are all around us. Suicide might be seen as the ultimate consequence; if our children cannot appreciate themselves, and their role in society, and their potential to improve their lives, they are easy victims for self-destruction. We allegedly have one of the highest youth suicide rates in the western world. Much has been written about the importance of self-esteem as an antidote, but perhaps there has been an oversight. It is not enough to make our children feel good about themselves; we have to actually provide them with practical tools so they can achieve success and happiness with their own hands. If you start out feeling good, but are continually frustrated by failure owing to ignorance, them self-esteem will not last anyway.

Other symptoms of ignorance are equally appalling. In countless small towns across North America we see young women who are young and vibrant at age fourteen, yet within a short decade, they are passing us on the same street, overweight, badly dressed in sloppy tracksuits, pushing a stroller. Worse, their eyes are dead. If a serial killer were stalking our communities, and killing even a handful of our daughters, we would rise up in fury. But let their minds die by the thousands, and we don't appear to notice. And it is not just the young mothers. The young fathers slouch their way along, their eyes dead under their baseball caps, a beer gut already hanging over their jeans, a sloppy sweatshirt proclaiming Chicago Bulls. These are not hasty judgements based upon superficialities such as clothes; the bodies merely reflect the minds. Many of these unfortunate men and women have been crippled every bit as much as if their parents had wrapped their tiny feet when they were babies.

Once we let ignorance take root and grow, our minds become both shallow and narrow. Our minds have shrunk as surely as a child with bound feet. The smaller our minds, the greater our misery. The smaller our minds, the fewer our opportunities in life. This is why so many different spiritual paths challenge us to develop a bigger view of the world. It was once popular to use "mind expanding" drugs for recreation; however foolish this may have been, it was none the less driven by a certain inspiration. An expanded mind is one that is fundamentally changed. A big mind cannot experience the world in the same way as a small one.

Our minds are naturally as vast as the summer sky. In this spacious world, the ordinary frustrations of life can rise and fall without knocking us off balance. There is enough space for us to feel our surges of anger, our bouts of depression, and our flashes of fear, without being overwhelmed by them. In the Buddhist tradition, the practice of meditation cultivates this sort of spacious mind. Sometimes we can be afraid of this mental space because we are not used to a certain relaxed feeling of emptiness, but as we learn to relate with spaciousness, we find that our awareness of life increases. We can actually just appreciate experiences as they arise. As we relax with the space, we find that our confidence and inspiration are naturally present.

This kind of spaciousness has nothing to do with being "spaced out." Being spaced out has the sense of being disoriented, of being unable to appreciate the details of our ordinary life. It has a quality of dullness. Being spaced out is another form of ignorance. When someone is spaced out, we can look into their eyes and see that there is a certain deadness.

With genuine spaciousness there is a sense of open sky above us and solid earth beneath our feet. Our minds are naturally attuned to each detail of our lives as experiences arise and fall away. We notice the sun rise in the east, we see the ice crystals on the window pane, we smell the hot morning coffee, we can take the time to greet our friends on the street; there is the time to do things properly. At the same time, we are not obsessive about all of these details. The sky-like quality of spaciousness gives us natural feeling of vision, an intuitive feel for life's great possibilities. The sense of vision and experience of space arise easily together. They just naturally fit into the big picture.

There is a quotation from the Bible that begins, "To every thing there is a season, and a time to every purpose under heaven"(Eccl. 3:1-8). The popularity of this passage extends from wall posters to coffee mugs to songs. Why should this particular text from an obscure section of the Bible have such broad appeal? It may be that it comes close to describing the natural spaciousness within us, the space within which all of life's aspects naturally arise and fall away. The passage describes an enlightened quality we already feel.

The absence of such awareness in many young parents is distressing. It is as if there is no vision about the possibilities for their lives, no awareness of the passing of time, no sense that life is precious and will end all too soon. We may be shocked that Asian parents can sell their son or daughter into a life of slavery making carpets. What we may fail to see is that allowing a child's naturally spacious and inquisitive mind to wither is just another way of turning them into a slave. A slave is a person with no power over his or her life. A victim is someone who is being hurt and cannot stop the pain. A prisoner is someone who is trapped and lacks the tools to escape. All around us on the street we can the eyes of slaves, victims and prisoners. When a baby is born and you look into its eyes, none of these are there. Where did they come from?

As parents we may have no more important task than to convey some sense of vision in life, some sense of spaciousness, some sense of a compassionate view of human affairs. If a child really cannot aspire to be anything more than a basketball player, our children and our society are doomed. As parents we have to show our children a bigger view of the world and their place in it. What might this entail? How can we inoculate our young against terminal ignorance?

1. **Knowledge of history**. History shows us both great monsters to fear and great saints to model ourselves after. If a child cannot image the monstrosity of a Stalin or Hitler, or the inspira-

tion of Ghandi or Martin Luther King, how can he appreciate what is going on around him? If instead of such images, a child knows only know Mickey Mouse, the Flintstones, hockey and baseball, how can he possibly make sense of his own life?

2. **Knowledge of laws and basics of good conduct**. Laws and decent conduct are the foundation of any ordered society. They are what prevent us from degenerating into the savagery of a Rwanda or Yugoslavia. A child needs to know how to behave in society, how we are governed, how our legal system works, and what it means to have rights and responsibilities within this system.

3. **Knowledge of human psychology**. We all feel pain, and we are all trying to find ways to become happy. If we cannot recognize the forces that arise in our life, how can we be a functional adult?

4. **Inspiration**. We do not have to accept things as they are. If we did, we would never have progressed from simple tribal apes. The inspiration to improve human conditions has produced everything from the drinking glass to the Space Shuttle. If children have no sense that they can improve themselves and improve the world, they are trapped.

The fundamental responsibility for parenting is to awaken within our child a sense of just how large the world is, and how many ways there are for them to contribute to human society. That is one reason why, in this short book, I deliberately have drawn upon historical and political examples far from our own time: the larger the scale of our thinking, the more naturally we begin to develop a certain perspective on our own lives. Perspective, as all artists know, requires space. If our knowledge of the past goes no farther back than our baby pictures, and no further ahead than next week's television schedule, how are we ever to make any sense of our lives? Yet this is all too often where we leave our children.

I have already told my children I will not take them to Disney World. It is not that a theme park is inherently evil in some dark way. Rather, for similar amounts of money, a family could travel to the vast Canadian north on the Polar Bear Express, they could canoe a mighty river, they could visit a half-dozen famous battle sites, they could see a rocket launched into space, they could watch the morning sun rise over a desert, they could hear the cries of the birds at night in a tropical rain forest, they could...well, the list is endless. These are all real things, all experiences that give us a sense of who we are and where we belong in space and time. In contrast, the theme park approach is to fill in our time with plastic models, cheap thrills, and a confused babble of messages that only disorient us further.

We are all trapped in confusion. We can aspire to wake up to a spacious mind that allows space for cultivating qualities such as compassion, steadfastness, gentleness, stewardship and responsibility. But it is not enough to just wake up ourselves. As we develop our sense of appreciation for the world, as we develop a certain sense of perspective, as our spaciousness matures, we can share the experience with our fellow human beings. Where better to start than with our children and our grandchildren? If not our own, there are countless children who desperately need an adult to whom they can relate. Who else will introduce them to the world if not ourselves? Our most important challenge as an adult is to help our children grow into good citizens with a natural sense of balance in their lives. Never will we have as much responsibility and power as when we hold a baby in our arms.

Revulsion

We should not be surprised when we are minding our own business, and unexpectedly find that we are increasingly immobilized by a sense of revulsion about our life. It may not be that we have a problem in quite the way we imagine we do. We could welcome this voice when we hear it. Maybe it is a warning that we are screwing things up. Throughout history people have had to grapple with the suspicion that something is wrong with their life. And yet it can be a shock when we find it happening to us.

How revulsion will manifest itself is impossible to say. Perhaps we will find that acts of arrogance on our part have wounded other people by making them feel fearful and inadequate. Perhaps we will experience a series of defeats that cause us to exclaim, "Why me, Lord?" Perhaps we suddenly find life so claustrophobic and predictable, so slug-like, that it cries out for some action. Perhaps our life has become so full of action and activity that it cries out for some peace and simplicity. Perhaps our loyalty and trust will be undermined when we are betrayed. Perhaps we become suddenly ill. Revulsion arises; who can say what caused it and what form it will adopt?

A common piece of Buddhist liturgy, and one that is recited each morning in many meditation centers, states, "Revulsion is the foot of meditation." That is to say, revulsion is an emotion that has a wisdom disguised in it. Revulsion is traditionally what brings people to the Buddhist path. Revulsion is like a red flag on the path of our lives—something is wrong, something is blocking the tracks ahead. Instead of reacting against revulsion, we could relax a little and give it the time to speak. We could see it as a voice from within that says we are not living our lives in a way that joins our hearts and our minds, that joins heaven and earth. If joy is an indicator that we are living life fully, revulsion is the red warning light on the instrument panel. We know what happens in cars if we continue to ignore the red light for oil pressure: the engine seizes.

We can remember that we are not alone when this happens.

Many people have felt revulsion like this in their lives. This is not to belittle revulsion, or our experience of it. Quite the opposite: when we hear it, the voice may be so deep, dark, painful and confused that it is difficult to understand. It may therefore be useful to know that some other people have gone through this. Let us look at a couple of examples. What did they find?

We meet Job in one of the oldest books in the Old Testament. He is a prosperous and faithful Hebrew man. But things change. Trials arrive, including the capture of his daughters by a marauding tribe, the loss of his farm animals, the murder of his servants, the collapse of a house upon his sons, and even an attack of boils covering his body. At first Job is accepting, but eventually he complains about the situation. God answers that since He is all-powerful and all-seeing, and created the universe in the first place, why should a mere human complain? We may find this Old Testament answer not very helpful. Just because God is all-powerful, does it give Him the moral right to torture someone weaker? This seems to be the philosophy of a bully. We may, nonetheless, catch an element of truth in God's answer. The universe is so large and complex and so far beyond our understanding and appreciation that we really have no reason to complain. A complaint against the universe, shaking our fist at the sky—such acts are pointless. One cannot complain about what is.

But acceptance is not necessarily the best answer to revulsion. Consider a Christian example, Saul of Tarsus, later called Paul. Saul is a zealous and self-righteous man, and is busily involved in the persecution of the early Christians. Apparently he is a man of action. He travels to Damascus as a part of his campaign against them. He has a vision on the road along the way. Today we might say he has a crisis of conscience or, in our terms, that he experiences revulsion. He is struck dumb for three days, and then ends up joining the disciples in preaching Christianity.

Finally, consider an example from the Buddhist tradition. Naropa was a great scholar in India who lived in the years following 1000 AD. Apart from being a respected citizen, he was married to a woman from a cultured Brahmin family. He seemed to have it made. Then, so the story goes, he met an ugly woman who cross-examined him about his knowledge. It became clear to him that while he had great intellectual skills, he had failed to appreciate their inner meaning, their heart. Naropa left to search for a teacher to show him the connection between heart and mind. He finally met Tilopa living in a shack, feeding on offal discarded by fishermen. Tilopa put him through a series of outrageous trials which were both embarrassing to a man of his reputation, and physically challenging to his body. These trials demolished his old habitual patterns and established him on the road to enlightenment. Naropa became a lineage holder of Tibetan Buddhism. Had he not experienced revulsion, he would never have started on this path.

We can watch for revulsion. Whether it is an inner voice, a light at night, or a real visit from an old woman, there is no point in pretending that revulsion is not there. It may take some time to decide what to do. I don't imagine that Naropa's scholarly colleagues, or his Brahmin parents-in-law, had anything good to say about his going on the road. Equally, it was likely difficult for Saul to explain to his superiors who were planning the persecution of Christians, that he had changed his mind.

One contemporary response to revulsion is therapy. We may need to be cautious. It is, of course, sometimes helpful, particularly if we need an objective advisor. But if we feel revulsion, the path of therapy could merely take us down the route of trying to blame someone for having created the pain in the first place. In the Buddhist tradition, we are advised that if we find an arrow in our heart, there is little value in speculating about who crafted it. Just pull it out. Or, our therapist may be intent on minimizing the pain enough that we can avoid examining its message. In such a case our high-priority message for self-examination might be treated as an inconvenience that prevents us from getting on with the business of earning, buying and owning.

We need to sit and look at our revulsion. But we do not want to get stuck in it. It is the foot of meditation, not the body, not the head. It is the beginning, and not the end.

Naiveté

Naiveté is easily misunderstood. Naiveté, like ignorance, is not merely a consequence of youth and inexperience. Nor is it just that one does not know. It is, rather, that one does not want to know.

Naiveté is a pure expression of the fear of seeing the world as it is. If we refuse to see the world nakedly, as it really is, without the embroidery of our own feelings, then we cannot be truly skillful and accomplished.

Our insight naturally shows us the world as it is. However painful this bright light of insight might occasionally feel, we must see the world clearly to express warriorship. But if our naiveté falls between us and the world, and blinds or confuses us, how can we aim our sword with care? How can we strike so as to disarm our foe without shedding blood, or better still, how can we parley and invite him to our side? Blindly, we struggle and fail. The knight with the visor that falls just as the enemy rides into view is not much use to have around; in fact, such a knight is a real danger to companions who are counting on his watchfulness. We doom ourselves by such blindness.

We experience naiveté in our life continually. There are at least two different aspects of naiveté. One is a heavy, dark form that just puts us to sleep. The conscious retreat from situations that threaten our world view. The worm-like withdrawal from painful truths. The poison gas that dulls our senses. There is also a more active, but subtle, form of naiveté. Shield-like, it leaps to cover us just as our hearts or eyes open to a flash of insight. The instinctive jerk of our hand to cover our eyes. It happens so quickly that we may not even notice that we are suddenly hidden behind armor or seeing the world through a dulling plastic visor.

In summary, the experience of naiveté is the experience of blinding ourselves. The consequences of naiveté are personal failure and harm to others. The origin of naiveté is our unwillingness to see the world as it is.

This does not mean we must see the worst in everything, and feed our natural cynicism. The cynic has merely built a suit of armor so thick that insight is obscured. Yet, strangely, in spite of the thick armor, the light of insight still sneaks in and it must be denied again and again.

Good things happen. Bad things happen. We experience them as they arise. We need not cling to them. But when we say "not clinging," we do not mean "not seeing." We are not turning ourselves into zombies, blind fools, brain-dead warriors. We do not close our eyes to the terrain; we take the high ground and, where possible, avoid the swamps. If we must walk through the swamp, we accept the damp and cold and leeches without complaint.

If we cannot relax and feel the nature of experiences as they arise, if we find that we are wrapping ourselves in naiveté, practice is required. There is no need to beat ourselves up. Rather, we can gently remain steadfast through painful experiences, frustrating experiences. A chink in our armor? Shock? Gradual spread of pain? Do we immediately seal the crack in our armor? Do we inject ourselves with morphine? Or do we see the light and feel the wound? If we inject ourselves with morphine each time the world pricks us, we may find we are unable to feel anything at all.

In our lives, the chasm of cynicism lies on one side, and the chasm of naiveté falls away on the other. With the clear, open sky above, we walk the razor's edge. Through the clouds and mist we follow the ridge top of awakened heart and mind. If we fall into the valley on either side, we climb up again. It will get easier. Eventually, we keep our balance.

Waking Up

Inspiration
Defeat
Death
Celebration
Liberation

•••

Inspiration

"I have a dream ..."

These words of Martin Luther King could inspire each of us. Inspiration. Vision. Dreams. Humans can be measured by the scale of their dreams. Inspiration is the fuel to improve the world. Inspiration is the realization that we need not be so cruel or stupid, that an enlightened society is possible. Inspiration has been the fuel of great social reformers and of all great exemplars of love and compassion.

Inspiration naturally expands our view of the world. When our mind shrinks to just ourselves, just our backyards, just our room in our parent's basement, just our office, inspiration can dissolve this view back into natural spaciousness. We see our place in the world, we see the confusion of others, we see the potential in the world, we see that others cannot see this potential, we are inspired to speak out about the opportunities that exist just before us.

Inspiration has a sense of sky, spaciousness, a king's view. To be effective it must be joined with earth, with solidity, with practicality, with a soldier's view. A favourite calligraphy of mine is called "Heaven, Earth and Man." It consists of three horizontal strokes joined by one vertical. The symbolism is clear. Humans (the middle stroke) are stretched between the vision of sky and the practicality of earth. Some feel only earth; they cannot lift their eyes out of the gutter to conceive that things could be better. They accept and wallow in their defeatism. Others see only sky; they are so full of their own vision as prophets that they cannot connect with earth, with practicality, or with their own hands. Our challenge is always to join sky with earth.

The world needs more prophets and dreamers now. It seems safe to say that we suffer from too little vision, that financial success is now the sole dream that we are expected to dream. Inspiration is an energy that can expand that vision, extend our horizons, create space for our minds and room for our hearts to grow. But if we do not use our inspiration, it withers. Too many have dismissed their dreams, have allowed them to wither, have given up on themselves and on the world.

Inspiration is not that easily lost, although it may become obscured and covered in dust. It is a natural quality that re-arises within us when we create the time and space in our lives. We practice simplicity, for example, in order to create the space that invites inspiration. If our inspiration seems limp, we could make a home for it. When it arrives, we could feed it. Then we could begin to exercise it. Consider the number of humans who are running, or lifting weights, or swimming to exercise their bodies. Can we not do as much for our inspiration?

A first expression of our inspiration might be to describe the vision. Humans are hungry for better possibilities; many feel the pain of claustrophobia. We can be inspired by those who can see visions and who can explain them. We could therefore be inspired to share our view with others. This might even be our duty; some of our fellow humans have seen their own visions wither as they age. Describing the vision is our first tool as leaders and creators. We must be able to vividly paint scenes and show them through our own acts.

Inspiration can, however, get too big for the space around it. A warning sign is that it makes us feel solid and full of ourselves. We may become attracted and then intoxicated by something that is actually harmful. The degree of our intoxication may prevent us from reconnecting with earth, from experiencing the practical consequences of our vision. We could wake up one morning convinced that we must convert everyone else to our particular view of the world. We could say, in this way, that the Grand Inquisitor was inspired to protect Catholicism from heresy, that Hitler was inspired to create the Third Reich, and that Stalin was inspired to create the world's largest system of concentration camps. Without knowing more about such men, it is difficult to say whether they were truly fueled by inspiration, or by fear, aggression, arrogance and hatred. But it appears that many others found them inspiring; otherwise they would not have acquired so much power. We can therefore see that evil may masquerade as inspiration. Do not rouse such men from the graves and put them at your helm. Watch for the warning signs. Real spiritual paths have real risks.

One guide we can trust is meditation. It provides us with the opportunity to look carefully at our instrument panel. The indicator we must always have one eye on is our heart, our compassion, our sadness. Compassion and sadness are good indicators that we are on the right course, that our engine is in good working order. When sadness and compassion are alive, the wind flows in though the cockpit and right through the front of our chest. We can allow ourselves to feel full of sadness that the world is so full of pain, that there is so much confusion, that there are so many missed opportunities for betterment of the human condition. We can watch for the red warning lights of fear, anger, frustration and aggression. Change your course if you see them. Never hesitate to pull into the pit stop and check the engine and the map. Most of all, watch the gauge of inspiration. If it is running low, stop and refuel.

Where do we find inspiration if it is depleted? Regular meditation may create the space for it to arise, but there is probably no better source than the words of other great humans who have triumphed over adversity to benefit others. Read their words. Have a shelf of their books near the bed. You could start with prophets and teachers. You could move on to social reformers and leaders. Make your own list of the ten that inspire you. Think of them when you are alone. Think of them when you face adversity. Rouse their image when inspiration seems withered. These people are the great warriors of the realm.

Visualize the great warriors who have preceded you. Strive to join their ranks. Fight at their side. Contemplate these words by Martin Luther King: "If a man hasn't discovered something that he will die for, he isn't fit to live."

Defeat

s we grow up, we begin to experience and accumulate defeats. Failed tests, waning friendships, lost loves, financial woes, hardships of many kinds. There may be painful mistakes on our part, such as misunderstanding our employer's expectations and losing our job. There may be unexpected obstacles such as disease, or simply failed brakes on a passing car. There may be consequences of acts that we realize were badly motivated or careless on our part. We become discouraged.

In reality, there cannot be life without obstacles. There cannot be campaigns without defeats. There cannot be humans without mistakes. Defeats should not be confused with failures. Contemplate this deeply.

At one level, we can, like a great general, review our defeats. What were our tactics, our strategies, our goals? How did they fail us? Who did we put in command? What were his weaknesses? Are there recurring problems in the chain of command, in the terrain we select for maneuver, in the courage of the troops, in the organization of the supplies, in the steadfastness of our commanders? We can study our defeats, and learn for the next time.

At another level, how can there be defeat at all? There is only the empty play of phenomena. The dance of the universe. Our bodies are made of elements formed in the hearts of dying suns. The light that touches our eyes at night may be a million years old and come from stars that are no longer there. Salt water of ancient oceans still flows in our arteries. Fossil stars, fossil light, fossil oceans. How can we fail in such a world? Only small mind, self-centered mind, egocentric view finds defeat. You see defeat. Is it? Is it? Is it not? Does it matter? Pleasure and pain, victory and defeat, all can be a pleasure to wear. Why do we cling to them at all?

Sometimes defeat is so raw that we can only lie bleeding while ravens pick the flesh from our fallen comrades. Pain. Sadness. Rawness. Desolation. There are times like this. Who can pretend otherwise? When life is like this, we may need to retreat, we may need time to heal, we may need The Witch of the Westmoreland to heal our wounds with goldenrod. If so, persevere on the path to her lair, but be gentle with yourself on the voyage.

Whatever happens in defeat, do not let your self get in the way. There are enough obstacles to fall over as it is. Where there is no self, there is no one to fail.

Death

Brothers and sisters this is a wonderful day to die.

What better motto for a warrior than this? I borrow it from a tribe of the First Peoples of North America. They once used to own this land. They were not afraid to talk of death.

But when we talk of death these days, we are often told not to be morbid. This creates confusion, because we cannot talk about anything worthwhile in life without facing death first. The denial of death is allied with ignorance, fear and anger.

Of course, those around us are afraid. What else can we feel when we do not know what lies ahead? We may think it is just better not to think about it. Like the monster in the closet, it will go away when the sun rises. Perhaps the first step to adulthood is to admit that it will still be there in the morning. We may think that if we hold tighter to our thoughts, or pump up our anger, or fall in love again, we can prove to ourselves we are still alive. We perhaps want to play a huge con job on ourselves; others will die, but we will live forever. A new car, a new house, a new job, a new spouse; all of these will prove to ourselves that we cannot die tomorrow. But we will—eventually.

How can a human live each day to the fullest, and yet plan for the future? Living in the face of death is not nearly as easy as it is to write the words. If we really are going to die tomorrow, it might seem pointless to put money in the bank, or start university. And yet, if we are going to live for eighty more years, perhaps it would be foolish to spend every last cent on a splendid party. We do not know which of these lies ahead, and so we live on the razor's edge. Like the Zen monk, we must clean the kitchen each night and put the rice to soak, just in case we wake in the morning. But we can appreciate the garden, and have a cup of sake at dusk, just in case we die tonight. It takes skill to ride the razor's edge without cutting off something important.

Illness also rouses our fear of death. We see what others experience, and fear that it will happen to us too. It will, one way or another. The sick person is like a sandwich sign with flashing lights at the main intersection: warning! Life is impermanent! You could be next! No wonder sick people make those around them uncomfortable. They want to live forever, and we remind them they cannot. But we are really all in the same boat: for all of us it is only a matter of time. Why quibble over a few decades in a billion years?

How are you, people ask? Not bad, I reply. It is easier to lie. Death hovers just out of reach, family life in chaos, job in peril, career disintegrating, friends fading, ambitions frustrated, talents wasted, body disobedient and mind in a dozen pieces—and yet I say "not bad"? Is this what Buddhists would call basic ignorance? Or just plain old secular basic stupidity? Or is it something else?

Dr. Sacks writes of the chemist with the brain tumor who discovers that nothing means anything to her any more. Her hands, a doorknob, a doctor, a relative—all of these things are still recognizable, but they all mean the same to her—nothing. At least pain and activity have a way of telling us that we are still alive. Perhaps the shadow of death means we should panic. Perhaps I should call my lawyer, write to my employer, phone the union, visit another doctor, pray, rub ashes on my skin, tear my clothes off and go screaming naked down the road. Not tonight, anyway; it is below zero and there is a strong north wind. Tomorrow perhaps. Sitting on a meditation cushion teaches us, if nothing else, that we cannot scratch every itch, cannot fidget to ease each irritation. Sit. Wait.

Death will come. If not tonight, then perhaps tomorrow. But our sons and daughters will go on. And if not ours, somebody else's. I can feel warm skin, feel breath on my arm as I write this late at night in bed (for they still climb into my bed around midnight). Airplane flies overhead on the way to the Ottawa airport. Occasional star. Emptiness. Out breaths, slightly out of phase. Except for the airplane, it might be night in a warm African Savannah, the young asleep in the trees.

A parent has to think about death. We fear for our children. Perhaps this is how we face our own fear of death. We are guardians, like the corvettes that used to guard the convoys sailing the North Atlantic oceans during the Battle of the Atlantic. Father is beside you, binoculars scanning the sky, alert for any threat, ever on watch for approaching death. We can flash messages to one another, but the radio keeps silence. Infrequent meetings of the minds across the waves. Icebergs float by. Seabirds of unknown kinds pass. Sometimes you seem distant, and I motion for you to stay closer—who knows what risks lurk outside the range of my guns? Sometimes we get too close and there is the screech of metal hulls grinding and the yells as we each blame the other for poor navigation, even as we really know it was just the wind and currents. We pull back before one of us is holed, and sail on. We carry with us the scars of such collisions, paint missing in great rusty streaks, but no structural damage, we hope. Some days are foggy and I can only guess roughly where you are. Other days are crisp and clear; your silhouettes stand out against the sub-Arctic sky. Occasional frantic activity—U boat ahead, and I circle tossing depth charges overboard, watching the sky anxiously for the dive bomber that might sink you. Images of men in the icy sea, burning fuel on the water, bodies in life rafts—bus running over you or pervert snatching you from the next aisle while I buy milk and juice.

At first we believe that we can guide our children into harbor, but of course this is not so. Rather it is that we must sail like this in convoy until separated in some storm, driven on diverging paths to unknown seas. Or until one of us lags behind; we cannot stop for stragglers, not on this ocean, not in this life, perhaps next time, it was good knowing you. Or until one of us slides beneath the icy waters leaving only an oil slick to temporarily calm the waves. The corvette must be ever resigned to going to the bottom first. We will all slip into the waves eventually. I feel that I was more than fortunate to share this portion of the voyage in spite of the complications, the engine failures, the storms, the arguments, the complaints. The morning sunrise over the ocean is still inspiring. The golden noon sun still shows the foam on the whitecaps. Dusk still has a faint blue tinge. Night has many stars.

Brothers and sisters, this will be a wonderful day to die. Today is a wonderful day to live. May you become great sea captains, compassionate masters of the Seven Seas and universal monarchs of unknown lands.

Meanwhile, man the watch at all times. Hold the wheel firmly but not too tightly. Keep your engines in good repair. Make sure the cook continues to serve hot biscuits and coffee even in the stormiest weather. Consult the ship's manual when you feel the need. Pull it out at night occasionally; refresh your memory for the days ahead. You must know the ship you sail.

Celebration

*L*ife passes. As it does, how many things there are to celebrate! There is the passing of the seasons: Summer Solstice, Winter Solstice, Spring Equinox, Fall Equinox. There are the changes of the seasons: snow melt, spring floods, leaves open, birds return, autumn harvest, leaves redden, leaves fall, first snow. There are the events of our lives: birthdays, marriages, births, wakes. There are victories: games won, exams with good grades, degrees, jobs, promotions, articles published. A life without celebration is like a sentence without punctuation. It is there, sprawled out before us, but even in the middle we are not quite sure what to make of it. Yet it seems that we are losing our ability to celebrate. I find it hard to lure colleagues away from the desk for lunch. Not once have we celebrated the publication of a colleague's paper or the receipt of a grant. Nor have we gone out to dinner after a promotion. We are always too busy.

Perhaps part of it has to do with a persistent and creeping form of what we might call secular Calvinism. We retain a barely conscious view, now largely without any particular religious or spiritual basis, that indulgence is wrong. What are we to make, then, of celebration, of time with friends, of fine food and good drink? Are they spiritual activities? Or are they mere distractions that we must struggle to overcome?

A problem seems to be that many of us raised in the West lack trust in ourselves; we believe instead in our basic badness, original sin. As a consequence, we start believing that self-denial and self-punishment are somehow spiritual. We may fear that celebration is just a first step down the path to overindulgence, gluttony, licentiousness, debauchery, Saturnalia. But from the enlightened point of view, such self-denial can just create more anger and rigidity. If self-hatred intoxicates us, our antidote is to relax and begin to makes friends with ourselves and, coincidentally, with the world. Perhaps we are not so bad as we think; perhaps the world is not so bad as we believe. Some sort of gentleness is necessary. Some sort of inquisitiveness is needed. Some sort of trust in the world is helpful.

Of course, the practice of celebration does not mean that we spend our nights in a drunken stupor, or that we spend our lives groaning from over-consumption like the Romans in Fellini's *Satyricon*. Perhaps these sorts of images, these caricatures of celebration, are part of our difficulty in working with the idea. Feasts have been a continual part of human experience; they originated no doubt when the tribe killed an elephant, and grew more rowdy when others figured out how to make fire and to brew beer. This tradition continued through the pageantry of the Middle Ages, right up to the Governor General's garden party. Still we have our suspicions.

This fear of celebration is not restricted to Christian and secular views. From the traditional Buddhist view, most of the suffering of human beings, and the disorder in society, is caused by addiction to psychological states such as ambition, arrogance, greed and anger; other addictions are similar in nature and effect. To continue to indulge in any destructive state, be it intoxication with anger or intoxication with alcohol, will bring only further pain to oneself and harm to others. We therefore begin with a foundation. We step onto the Buddhist path by renouncing habitual intoxication to harmful emotions and cultivating right conduct, moderation, simplicity, and generosity. Some people interpret this to mean that the only way to be a Buddhist is to be a strict vegetarian, to renounce alcohol, perhaps even to drink only herbal tea while sitting cross-legged on the floor of an untidy apartment. Perhaps a red cushion is too boisterous; maybe it should be black. Maybe even a meditation cushion is too indulgent; perhaps we should just sit on an old sweater, or even on the floor.

But renunciation is only a tool. At some point the path expands; we begin opening up to the world. Tantric Buddhist mediation masters have often scandalized their contemporaries by participating in all manner of outrageous activities such as feasts and celebrations. My own teacher, Chogyam Trungpa Rinpoche, was legendary in this regard. It is quite remarkable how many people still worry about what they perceive as scandalous behavior on his part. Apparently they would have been quite happy to sit at his feet drinking herbal tea and admiring his robe. We might aspire to a more spacious view of the spiritual path. Chogyam Trungpa was constantly encouraging his students to let go of conventional views of renunciation and spirituality. He constantly encouraged students to appreciate the ordinary, to find the sacred in basic householder's life. We can learn from Tantric masters like him to relax in our discipline, to dance instead of fighting with the phenomenal world.

This book has made ongoing reference to the practice of warriorship. The Shambhala path has been a reference point in these essays. This secular path of meditation, using the analogy of warriorship, begins by working with basic gentleness, openness, non-aggression and unconditional confidence. The path, however, also expands to appreciation of the phenomenal world. This can include appreciation of single-malt scotch, Mozart, fiddle music and fine French cuisine, as well as sake, ikebana, Zen archery and ballet.

No beginner on these paths should think that mere overindulgence is an enlightened act, or even a spiritual practice. But then, neither should they think that refusing to drink the wine and insisting upon a glass of milk or ice water is any better. Celebrate the wine when there is wine; drink the water when there is water. Could it be any simpler? This is why meditation is important. As we begin working with our own state of mind through meditation, we begin to discover the enlightenment inherent in each of our daily activities.

There is a continual contrast in our lives between the experience of enlightened mind, and the more familiar confusion. Using the vehicle of meditation, we work with this contrast between awakened mind and cloudy mind. This contrast inspires us to explore further. We discover that sacredness can arise as an ongoing experience whether we are cleaning toilets, riding on the bus, opening a fine bottle of wine or sitting on a meditation cushion. Of course, if it were easy to wake up out of our habitual confusion by cleaning toilets or drinking wine, we would all have discovered enlightenment already. It is not quite that easy. That is why there are (and have been for thousands of years) meditation teachers and meditation centers. That is why there are instructions and guidance available.

Mark the seasons, punctuate your life, refresh your senses with celebration. Know a good wine from a cheap plonk, know plain fare from Epicurean. Eat, drink and be merry. Join celebration with meditation. Share your realm with others. Wake up to a king's view of the world.

Liberation

Death, celebration, liberation. We are nearing the end of these instructions. Ultimately, we take our place in the world and exercise our powers. Make friends with yourself. Know how to rule your world. Never forget your compassion for others. Always remember our motto of peace, order and good government.

Liberation, you ask? Are we there yet? What can a student, a lawyer, a teacher, a mechanic, a consultant, an artisan, a musician, a warrior, a knight, be liberated from? It is time for the test.

Test

Reconsider the instructions on self-control and simplicity. Choose a night when it is twenty degrees below zero with a strong north wind. Go for a walk. When you come to a red light, and the street is empty, watch yourself. Do you stand there and wait for the light to change, or do you rush across without a second thought?

You walked? Sorry, you fail. Go back to basic practices and

work with steadfastness. Try again next winter. Watch out for the boy on the skateboard. There are many seasons to come.

You waited? Good work. You pass. This is what self-discipline is all about. This is a warrior's secret weapon. Polish it regularly. Use it well.

Now go and find yourself a teacher to liberate you from being too damn stupid to get out of the cold. Show more compassion for yourself. As you search for a teacher, trust your own wisdom, believe in your own heart. At the same time, trust your skepticism, believe in your own unconditioned wisdom. Will you find your teacher wandering in the desert, living in a shack eating fish guts, drinking sake in a sushi bar in New York, or living in an apartment in Halifax? How should I know? Traditionally it is said that a teacher only appears to us when we have trained to the point where we are ready. Otherwise, the teacher may seem to be only a dead dog or a demon. When Naropa first saw his teacher, she appeared as an old woman. We may have to be patient. Whenever the teacher appears, he or she is only an outer manifestation of the guru within. Ultimately the world is our teacher. We are in a dance with the cosmos. Once we find someone to teach us the basic steps, we may have to improvise.

A warrior rules with a consort on one side and a trusted advisor on the other. He or she can listen to their counsel, but alone must take the responsibility for ruling with wisdom. May you have victories to celebrate and banquets to host. May our children inherit a better world for your efforts. Teach them the art of warfare, the art of gentleness, and the art of celebration.

Appendix

From START WHERE YOU ARE: A GUIDE TO COMPAS-SIONATE LIVING by Pema Chödron, ©1994. Reprinted by arrangement with Shambhala Publications, Inc., 300 Massachusetts Avenue, Boston, MA 02115.

SHAMATHA-VIPASHYANA MEDITATION

In shamatha-vipashyana meditation, we sit upright with legs crossed and eyes open, hands resting on our thighs. Then we simply become aware of our breath as it goes out. It requires precision to be right there with that breath. On the other hand, it's extremely relaxed and extremely soft. Saying, "Be right there with the breath as it goes out," is the same thing as saying, "Be fully present." Be right here with whatever is going on. Being aware of the breath as it goes out, we may also be aware of other things going on—sounds on the street, the light on the walls. These things may capture our attention slightly, but they don't need to draw us off. We can continue to sit right here, aware of the breath going out.

But being with the breath is only part of the technique. These thoughts that run through our minds continually are the other part. We sit here talking to ourselves. The instruction is that when you realize you've been thinking you label it "thinking." When your mind wanders off, you say to yourself, "Thinking." Whether your thoughts are violent or passionate or full of ignorance and denial; whether your thoughts are worried or fearful, whether your thoughts are spiritual thoughts, pleasing thoughts of how well you're doing, comforting thoughts, uplifting thoughts, whatever they are, without judgment or harshness simply label it all "thinking," and do that with honesty and gentleness.

The touch on the breath is light: only about 25 percent of the awareness is on the breath. You're not grasping or fixating on it. You're opening, letting the breath mix with the space of the room, letting your breath just go out into space. Then there's something like a pause, a gap until the next breath goes out again. While you're breathing in, there could be some sense of just opening and waiting. It is like pushing the doorbell and waiting for someone to answer. Then you push the doorbell again and wait for someone to answer. Then probably your mind wanders off and you realize you're thinking again—at this point, use the labeling technique.

It's important to be faithful to the technique. If you find that your labeling has a harsh, negative tone to it, as if you were saying, "Dammit!," that you're giving yourself a hard time, say it again and lighten up. It's not like trying to down the thoughts as if they were clay pigeons. Instead, be gentle. Use the labeling part of the technique as an opportunity to develop softness and compassion for yourself. Anything that comes up is okay in the arena of meditation. The point is, you can see it honestly and make friends with it.

Although it is embarrassing and painful, it is very healing to stop hiding from yourself. It is healing to know all the ways that you're sneaky, all the ways that you hide out, all the ways that you shut down, deny, close off, criticize people, all your weird little ways. You can know all that with some sense of humor and kindness. By knowing yourself, you're coming to know humanness altogether. So when you realize that you're talking to yourself, label it "thinking" and notice your tone of voice. Let it be

compassionate and gentle and humorous. Then you'll be changing old stuck patterns that are shared by the whole human race.
Compassion for others begins with kindness to ourselves.

For further information on meditation
or programs in your area, contact:

Shambhala International
1084 Tower Road,
Halifax, Nova Scotia
Canada B3H 2Y5
(902) 425-4275

About the Author

Paul Keddy is a professor at the University of Ottawa where he teaches and does research in Ecology. He was born in London, Ontario, but his father was in the armed services, so he traveled around Canada, living for a time as far west as Edmonton and as far east as Halifax. He is now married with two sons and, with his wife Cathy, lives amidst the forests of Lanark County, Ontario. He is thus thoroughly North American in outlook. At the same time, Dr. Keddy has taken vows in both the Buddhist and Shambhala traditions, and has taught at the Ottawa Shambhala Centre for some years. He believes that the path introduced in this book provides a means for us to reconnect with the inherent spirituality in everyday life without rejecting western civilization and without fearing our day-to-day life circumstances.

Dr. Keddy began the study and practice of the Buddhist path in the late 1970s. He was impressed by its logical consistency, its deep concern for the problem of human suffering, and its emphasis upon personal experience rather than faith. In 1982, when he moved to Ottawa, he became a student of the Tibetan Buddhist meditation master Chogyam Trungpa Rinpoche, being attracted not only by the clarity of his teaching, but by Chogyam Trungpa's courage in living an unconventional and yet thoroughly western lifestyle. The foundation of this book lies in the Shambhala teachings he received from Chogyam Trungpa, which present a traditional spiritual path in a context that is contemporary. The emphasis is upon appreciating, rather than rejecting, our day-to-day experiences as they arise. Noticing how we are imprisoned by our hopes and fears gives us our first glimpse of something more spacious in the human condition. This book further draws upon examples from Dr. Keddy's Christian upbringing, from Zen, and from his further study with Sakyong Mipham Rinpoche and Sonam Rinpoche, meditation masters now living in Canada.

The more difficult the times become, the more need there is for such teachings, and the more powerful they become. We can use adversity as well as pleasure as a means to *wake up*—which, Dr. Keddy adds, is just as well, since life seems to bring everyone more than their fair share of adversity.

"Good and bad, happy and sad, all thoughts vanish into emptiness like the imprint of a bird in the sky."

Chogyam Trungpa Rinpoche